The Australian Indigenous Peoples

Bushtucker

Etiquette - Dreaming - Magick

By Rev. Dr S. D'Montford et al.

TABLE OF CONTENTS

IN THE BEGINNING	8
INDIGENOUS ETIQUETTE	**10**
TERMINOLOGY	10
GREETINGS	10
MALE & FEMALE CULTURAL ROLES	11
TRANSPARENCY	11
EYE CONTACT	11
QUESTIONS	11
NATIONAL COSTUME	12
RESPECT FOR THE DEAD	13
THE ORUNCHA SPIRIT MEN	13
KADICHA	15
AUSTRALIAN INDIGENOUS SERVICE DURING WAR	17
POLITICAL MANIPULATION OF INDIGENOUS PEOPLE	19
RESEARCH INTO INDIGENOUS PREHISTORY	21
POPULATION "Y"	34
RESPECT FOR BUNYIPS, YOWIES & MI MI	36
Yowies	36
Bunyips	38
The MiMi	40
Totems	41
THE KOOKABURRA TOTEM	**43**
THE BUTTERFLY TOTEM	**47**
THE SWAMP	48
SPIRIT GUIDES	50
GHOSTS	52
THE WHITE GODDESS	54
INDIGENOUS CREATION STORY	55
THE DARK GODDESS	57
BIRTH OF THE BUTTERFLIES	59
THE PSYCHE	61
1. Nurture Yourself – Nurture The Young. 62	
2. Create Your Own Safe Haven 62	
3. Strive To Be Your Own Ideal 62	
4. Stretch Your Wings Cautiously 62	
5. Taste Life With Your Feet 63	
6. Care For Yourself 63	
THE BUTTERFLY'S ULTIMATE LESSON	63
AUSTRALIAN BUSH TUCKER	**65**
WARNING!	65
NATIVE FRUITS & VEGGIES	**65**
WARRIGAL SPINACH	65
Spinach Soup	65
MACADAMIA NUTS	66
WATTLE	66
Wattle Billie Tea	67

BUNYA NUT	**67**
Bunya Mash	67
Bunya Toffee	68
BUSH TOMATO	**68**
Desert Tomato Soup	70
BOAB TREE	**70**
Roasted Boab Fruit and Seeds	71
LILLYPILLY	**71**
Lillypilly Vinegar	71
RIBERRY	**72**
Riberry Sauce	72
MUNTRI (Kunzea)	**72**
Native Muntri Sauce	73
PIGFACE	**73**
Pickled Pigface	73
ROSELLA FLOWER	**74**
Rosella Jam	74
QUANDONG	**75**
Stewed Quandongs	76
NATIVE HERBS AND SPICES	**77**
Native Peppers	77
Lemon Aspen	77
Lemon Myrtle	77
Paperbark	77
Green Gum-Tree Sticks	77

FISH & SEAFOOD — 78

NATIVE SEAFOOD DELICACIES	**78**
Australian Rock Oysters	78
Bugs	78
PIPIS	**78**
Pipi Chowder	78
CRABS	**79**
Blue Swimmers and Beer	79
MUSSELS	**79**
Mussels, Rice and (Bush) Tomatoes	80
PRAWNS	**80**
Grilled Prawns with Native Citrus	80
Waste Not Want Not	**81**
BARRAMUNDI	**81**
Barramundi in Paperbark	81
Whole Barramundi in Coals	82
SALMON	**82**
Salmon over coals	82
Poached Camp Salmon	82
TROUT	**82**
Trout in the Mud	83
MULLET	**83**
Mullet in Banana Leaves Over Coals	84
TiLAPIA	**84**
CROCODILE	84
Slightly Gum-Smoked Crocodile	85

YABBIES & CRAYFISH	**86**
YABBIES	**86**
Yabbie Cooking	86
Yabbies Served on Gum Leaves	86
Skewered Yabbies	87
CRAYFISH	**87**
Char-Grilled Crayfish	87
MARRON	**87**
Marron Nibbles	88
POULTRY	**89**
EMU	**89**
Barbecued Emu	89
Emu Egg Scramble	89
AUSSIE BREAD	**90**
DAMPER	**90**
Basic Damper	90
Aussie Beer Bread	90
Lemonade Scones	90
RED MEAT	**92**
BUFFALO	**92**
Rough Red Buffalo Steaks	92
Hot Coal Steaks with Native Peppercorns	93
Aussie Shovel Burgers	93
PRESERVING MEAT IN THE BUSH	**93**
Smoking 93	
Jerky 94	
Backyard Buffalo Jerky 94	
KANGAROO	**94**
Kangaroo Tail Soup	95
Roasted Kangaroo Leg	95
Kangaroo Rissoles	96
RABBITS	**96**
Kentucky Fried Rabbit	97
SMALLER THINGS	**98**
BOGONG MOTHS	**98**
Coolamon Moth Nuts	98
Macadamia Pop	98
WITCHETTY GRUBS	**98**
Witchetty Soup	99
HONEY ANTS	**99**
Honey Ant Bubble Tea	99
CAMP OVEN COOKING	**100**
CAMP OVEN CARE	**100**
PAPER TEST FOR OVEN TEMPERATURE	**100**
INDIGENOUS WORDS & LANGUAGE	**101**
Body parts	**102**
Kin relationships	**103**
Human classifications	**103**

Language, mythology, ceremony	104
Food, cooking and fire	104
Pieces of equipment	105
Landscape	106
Natural Items	106
Reptiles	106
Local animals	107
Birds	107
Fish & Sea Life	108
Plants	108

INDIGENOUS WRITTEN LANGUAGE 109
PROTO-WRITING CORRELATES TO INDIGENOUS CAVE "ART" 114
A WORD ON COOK'S MAPPING OF AUSTRALIA 119
IN THE END 124

All images of indigenous people in this book are either illustrations or pictures on display elsewhere – used with permission and respect by a not-for-profit organisation to discuss educational topics – —with complete honour and respect to the ancestors –

COVER IMAGES:
Background – Royalty Free Artwork by Pilbara on Pixabay
Inset: Food Desert bush tucker, Food, Berries Royalty Free Artwork by Penny Ash Pixabay
Inset: Painting -Australian Oruncha, High Medicine Man, wearing his magick markings, set against artwork from the Carnarvon Gorge main track Northern Territory. Authors own digital artwork. (see page 12 for details)

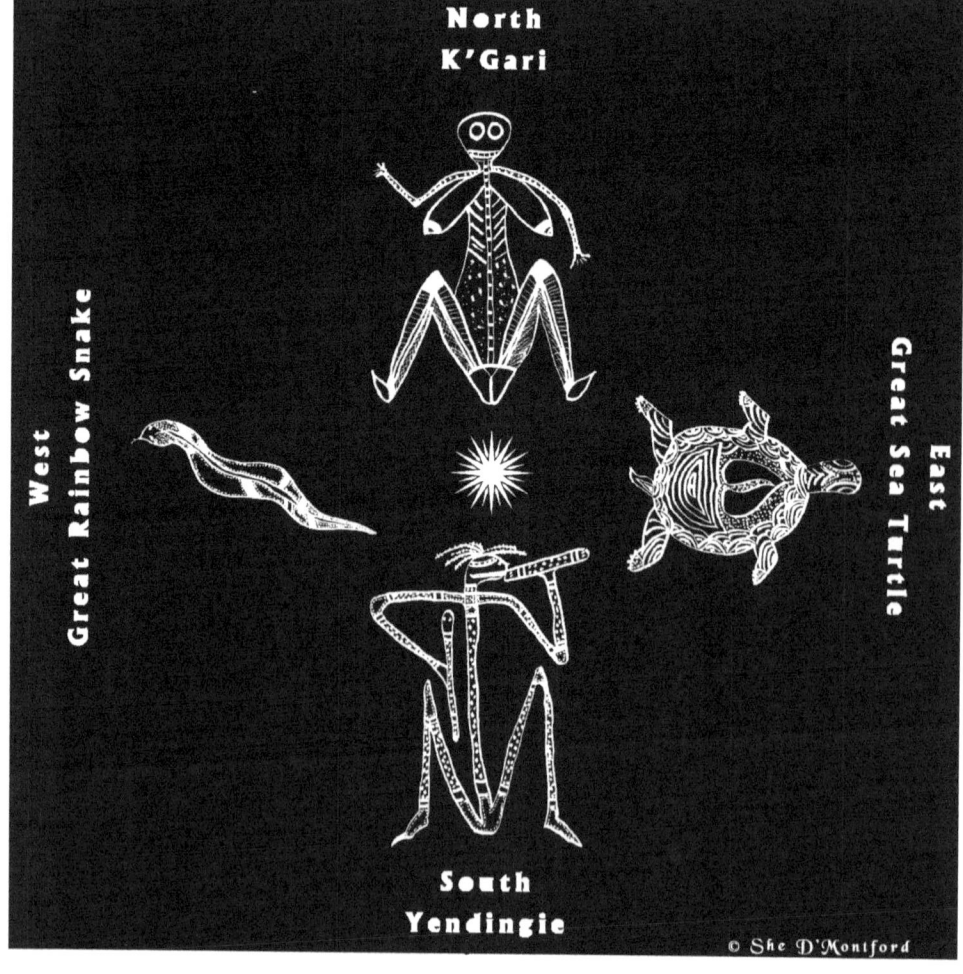

THE HAPPY MEDIUM PUBLISHING COMPANY
THE MESSAGE IS IN THE MEDIUM

Brings you: -**The Australian Indigenous Peoples Bushtucker Etiquette - Dreaming - Magick**

ISBN: 978-0-9943541-8-1

ebook: 978-0-9943541-9-8

Shé D'Montford's "**The Australian Indigenous Peoples Bushtucker Etiquette - Dreaming - Magick**" written by, cover design and layout Rev. Dr. S. D'Montford. Cover photography Spence & Gilles Royalty Free. © Copyright Rev, Dr S. D'Montford, Monday 5 February 2024, Gold Coast, Australia. Published by **THE HAPPY MEDIUM PUBLISHING COMPANY** for educational purposes.

ALL RIGHTS RESERVED. The information presented is protected under the Berne Convention for the Protection of Literature and Artistic Works, other international conventions, and national copyright and neighbouring rights laws. Extracts of the information in this book may be reviewed but not reproduced or translated without express written permission from the publisher. Reproducing or translating portions of this publication requires explicit, prior authorisation in writing. **Disclaimer:** The primary reason for this publication is entertainment and education about Pagan practices. While The Happy Medium Publishing Company and Shambhallah Awareness Centre have used all reasonable endeavours to ensure the information in this book is as accurate as possible, it gives no warranty or guarantee that the material, information, or publications made available by them are fit for any use whatsoever and require that you use your own common sense in working with any materials provided **THE HAPPY MEDIUM PUBLISHING COMPANY,** Shambhallah Awareness Centre and Rev. Dr S. D'Montford accepts no liability or responsibility for any loss or damage whatsoever suffered as a result of direct or indirect use or application of any material, publication or information obtained from them. **THE HAPPY MEDIUM PUBLISHING COMPANY** is a division of Shambhallah Awareness Centre, a tax-exempt Pagan Church, and a not-for-profit organisation. P.O. Box 3541, Helensvale Town Centre. Q. 4212 http://www.shambhallah.org Special Thanks to:- Ken Wills & Don Nikkelson and all the people who contributed to this work.

Image Credits - All images sent to me are credited where possible. Some have been sent to me anonymously for publication in the magazines over the years or have just been handed to me at festivals or during readings. If you now wish to be credited for these images, drop us a line, and I will credit you. Some images qualify as fair use under copyright law, such as use rationale, a low-resolution image from a publicly available copyright-free source used for critical commentary and discussion by a non-profit organisation for educational purposes. Any other uses of these images may be copyright infringement. Quotes in this book qualify as "fair use" under copyright law as "use rationale" used for critical commentary and educational discussion by a non-profit organisation. Any other uses of these quotes may be copyright infringement. All other images are from public domain sources.

IN THE BEGINNING

Indigenous Australians did not use the term "Aborigine" to refer to themselves, which comes from the Latin word ab, meaning "from the beginning." Before the arrival of non-Aboriginal people, they simply referred to each other as The People.

This text will refer to indigenous people as just that, those who are descended from the indigenous ancestors of this land.

The Dreamtime is the Australian indigenous belief system that explains the creation of the world and its significant stories. It is the foundation of knowledge which led to the laws of existence. To survive, these rules must be followed.

The Dreaming is the cultural history of the ancestor beings who emerged from the earth at the time of creation, told through oral traditions, paintings, and dance. Indigenous elders hate anthropologists who try to tell them about their own spiritual beliefs. There have been many books written on 'Aboriginals.' There is only one person's writings that comes close. Their own! This is written from personal connection, experience and love. There's a difference between a historian approaching knowledge at a distance and one who walks the path and documents it. Here are find indigenous concepts put into terms Western pragmatists can understand.

The beginning of existence was a two-dimensional world that was flat, dark and silent. However, when the sun illuminated the land for the first time, the supernatural Totemic Ancestor Beings forcefully broke into the third dimension of matter from beneath the ground. They roamed the barren surface of the world, changing their forms as they hunted and fought. During their travels, they created the landscape, and each feature of it tells their story, which is also our story. The decisions they made resulted in everything.

All of the natural elements, such as water, air, fire, the sun, the moon, the stars, and every living creature, rose from their decisions, both good and bad. This includes all food plants, ants, grasshoppers, emus, eagles, crows, parrots, wallabies, kangaroos, lizards, snakes, and more. Eventually leading to the creation of humans. Therefore, we are all descendants of the Dreamtime ancestors. All life today, whether human, plant, animal, bird, or fish, is part of a network of relationships that can be traced back to the great spirit ancestors of the Dreamtime.

As the ancestors grew tired from all their activity, they retreated back under the ground and returned to their sleep-like state, the dreaming. Some spirits transformed into rocks and trees or became part of the landscape. These places were considered sacred and held unique qualities.

The significance of The Dreamtime continues to be essential to all Australians today. Indigenous ceremonies that reenact the events of the ancient era of creation through art, dance, song, and chants, accompanied by the didgeridoo or clap sticks and the wisdom of the elders that recounts the story of early times, bringing the power of The Dreaming into modern life. However, many modern indigenous people have either abandoned their traditional beliefs or do not have knowledge of their own Dreamtime lore.

It's common for people to get confused by the wide range and diversity of Aboriginal and Torres Strait people. Most don't speak their traditional languages but may be fluent in many others. These people come from all walks of life. While traditional hunters still exist, there are also Indigenous doctors of philosophy. The range of skin colours is vast, from some of the darkest skin tones on the planet to the very fair. Interestingly, many Indigenous children from traditional communities in northwestern Australia are born with blonde hair and blue eyes, darkening as they age due to a sprinkling of Viking DNA. The lesson for both non-Indigenous and Indigenous people is not to stereotype others and to remember that people are different, regardless of their race.

Many indigenous elders welcome those born in this country but whose ancestors came from other lands. Those who are open to embracing this land's diverse and enchanting cultural history and who show it the respect it deserves will be remembered by future generations as their ancestors. They will pass down the traditions and values to the children of the future, ensuring that they are carried on for generations to come.

If you hold the following five statements dear to you, then you are welcomed On Country and embraced by the people.

1. 'We don't own the land; the land owns us.'
2. 'The Land is my mother; my mother is the land.'
3. 'The land is our food, our culture, our spirit and identity.'
4. 'We don't have boundary fences; we have spiritual connections.'
5. 'Land is the beginning and the end. It is where we start, and it is where we will ALL go'

INDIGENOUS ETIQUETTE

Different cultures have different customs that dictate their manners. Things we see as inoffensive can be very offensive to another culture and vice versa. As invited guests in someone else's country, it is wise to learn some indigenous etiquette to be mannerly and respectful to our hosts. This will outline some basic indigenous etiquette to help prevent social faux pas.

TERMINOLOGY

Due to 'politically correct' madness, gone are the days when you could call a spade a spade and a black fella a black fella! The truth is that, unlike African/Americans, most of our indigenous people are not that sensitive about what they are called unless it is said in a deliberately derogatory way.

However, the term "Indigenous" is preferred to "Aboriginal" when using a word to describe the first peoples of Australia collectively.

Traditional custodianship of an area is much more confined. There are over 200 Australian indigenous races/language groups that still exist. These can be thought of similarly to all the different nations and languages occupying Europe. All are quite different, though all can be broadly called European. It is incorrect to call these nations/language groups "tribes." The accepted term for identifying an individual group is "Mob."

To say, "What is your mob?" or "What mob are you from?" is the preferred form. Though Western sensibilities do not feel this is a respectful form of the question, as the term 'Mob' is used to describe a group of kangaroos, most indigenous groups appreciate its honesty rather than stumbling through attempts at political correctness that only set up a verbal image of their people as being an inferior minority group.

GREETINGS

As you are coming on to traditional country it is your responsibility to identify yourself first. The correct form is:-
1. State your name,
2. What you are to your people,
3. Where you are from and
4. What do you want to do here?

Example: "Greetings Aunty. ("Aunty" is a term of respect if they are an elder or "Uncle" for men if they are an elder – if you are not sure, then say "Greetings.") I am Sally Jones, a mother of four from North Sydney. I have come to accept your invitation to come On Country to share culture with you."

With any matriarchal mob, it is essential that all the males are highly respectful to the older women. Guys, please call all the older women or any woman sharing spiritual knowledge "Aunty."

MALE & FEMALE CULTURAL ROLES
Though our culture has been conditioned to see gender-assigned roles and taboos as discriminatory, the many indigenous mops have some very clearly defined women's and men's business. Some of these will be shared with you. Out of respect, these must not even be discussed with those of the opposite sex.

Women's sacred sites are for women only, and men's sacred sites are for men only. Any breach of this etiquette will result in the offender being asked (or forcibly removed) from the traditional lands on to which you have been invited.
Yes, spears and didgeridoos are men's business – clap sticks, coolamons, and digging sticks are women's business. In traditional culture, if you touched a tool of the other sex's business, you could be speared to death.

TRANSPARENCY
When someone from an indigenous culture asks you questions, it is essential that you be transparent and honest. Any perceptible avoidance, misdirection, deceit, unwillingness to answer or hiding something, will lose you respect. Traditionally, this is seen as a threat. These days, indigenous people rarely say anything. If these things are detected, they have less to do with you, or they will just not tell you the truth.

EYE CONTACT
Staring at someone from a traditional indigenous culture can be perceived as a threat and is considered rude. However, when questions or clarification are asked, meeting the gaze honestly and openly is appreciated. Never allow this to become threatening in any way, as it is felt that some of the soul can be stolen from the eyes.

QUESTIONS
Try not to ask questions, especially spiritual ones. It is considered rude to ask any question where there is a possibility that the questioned may not know the answer as the questioned then feels an obligation to give an answer. This puts them in a difficult position if they don't know the answers. If they don't know the correct answer, they may make

something up, as it is considered rude not to give you an answer when you ask for one. However, this often offends Western sensibilities but is intended to be polite and as helpful as possible, not deceptive.

If you ask spiritual questions, the possibility of duel offence and breach of etiquette is very real for two reasons:-

1) Many individuals from indigenous cultures have lost their traditional beliefs and their elders are attempting to spiritually re-educate as many of them as wish it. This is one of the things that has opened the way for us. The elders are willing to share some things with us who wish to be Gubberigional (i.e. white but learning indigenous ways) to prevent them from being lost if their young people remain fascinated with rap or African/American culture. We will be able to help preserve it for when they wish to return to it.

2) There are generally four levels of spiritual teaching within most mobs. Some things are exclusive within the different levels. Any level will rarely know it all. Each plays their part when needed and is not questioned about it.

If they wish to share voluntarily with us, that is permitted. So, even though you will be super-keen to learn as much as possible, allow the spiritual sharing to happen naturally and organically.

NATIONAL COSTUME
The Australian indigenous national costume is nothing! Dressing that way was seen as polite. It demonstrated that you have nothing to hide from those you wish to interact with. Things have changed, and in this matter, our cultural morés has been imposed, so it is unlikely that you will encounter any who are traditionally dressed.

Culturally, we are taught that being naked is a shameful, dishonourable thing, yet to the indigenous, wearing nothing was a way to prove how honourable you were. This one cultural etiquette contradiction highlights the many opposing traditions in our cultural differences. It reminds me of the biblical account in Genesis chapter 4 of the people of the land of Nod, east of Eden, who knew no shame or sin but later learned these from the descendants of Cain.

There is a slight possibility that you may encounter some who participate in the indigenous national dress. If you do encounter any people dressed in traditional indigenous costume (no matter what colour their skin is), try not to make any who choose to feel ashamed.

RESPECT FOR THE DEAD
Each Australian language group will have a set morning period for their dead, after which they dispose of all photos and personal belongings of that person. Then, they get on with life as usual. They completely let them go and do not call them back, just in case they disturb their journey towards rebirth.

This is the reason most Australian indigenous mobs refuse to look at photos of their departed. They feel that if the spirit senses them in pain from missing them, the spirit will put their journey of rebirth on hold and return to try to care for their grieving loved ones. All pictures used of indigenous people in this publication are royalty-free images sourced from very public sources (i.e. museums, war memorials etc.) As these images are already publicly used and discussed, the damage has already been done. So, let's utilise their pictures for some good.

Additionally, they never use the same word as the departed one's name, just in case they feel they are being called back. If he/she were called "Kangaroo", they would invent another word in their native tongue to replace it. This is why each indigenous language group is so complicated and ever-changing.

To get to aboriginal heaven, dead indigenous individuals must travel around the song lines of their mob's land, i.e. the seasonal pathways through their ancestral lands. They have to reach the body of water that is most sacred to their mob. It can be a billabong, a river or the ocean. Once there, the spirit changes into a little tadpole or tiny fish playing merrily in those waters. When their new mother goes into that water for a swim, they will swim up inside her to be reborn. (And they knew this without the use of an electron microscope.)

Building homes on lay lines or aboriginal song lines can result in spiritual through traffic, which is not dangerous, but it can wake you up in the middle of the night. There are ways of diverting it around the house. These lines most often follow groundwater or ridge lines. Digging a copper cable around the corner of the house that bisects this line can divert spiritual traffic around the home rather than cutting through someone's bedroom.

THE ORUNCHA SPIRIT MEN
This image is a painting of an indigenous Arrernte Oruncha man in the South Australian Museum, from the book "Peoples of the World," by Walter Spencer and Francis Gillen. The image depicts him projecting magick crystals into a patient's body. The Oruncha man had magic crystals inserted under his skin during his initiation, which allowed him to

perform this healing ritual. He wears a hand-painted ochre design on his head, representing his relationship to his totem, the Rainbow Serpent. Leaves partly hide the design, but it is an essential symbol of his spiritual power. The vertical black line is himself. The circles around it represent the crystals under his skin, radiating energy. He also wears a kangaroo thighbone through his nose. All his sacred objects are called Churinga.

The Oruncha Spiritmen live in sacred caverns, and the Kadicha visit them when necessary. It is believed that they were responsible for creating most of the cave paintings found in sacred places. These paintings served as signposts, warnings, dreaming lore, and initiation degrees. They were a form of active language that allowed for communication, and those who created them could move between men's and women's business and between different groups and nations. The Kadicha were the physical representatives who lived amongst the people, moving freely where they liked.

The Oruncha are more spiritual than physical and generally stay hidden. Kadicha were the priests, judges, and executioners and were feared more than respected. The Oruncha are equivalent to a Pope in their spiritual authority and are respected for their power. They can initiate other spiritual levels within the traditional indigenous system, such as the Kadicha, the Lore Keepers, and the Healers.

The Indigenous believe that most of these powerful men of high degree had merged back into the spirit realm by the 1930s. Their surviving sacred objects, including the Churinga, can be found scattered through museums in Australia.

KADICHA
Donald William Nikkelson, or **Donnie Didge** as he is affectionately known, is the Regional Aboriginal and Torres Strait Islander Citizen Of The Year Award Winner for 2013.

The indigenous still have Magick men that they call "Clever Fellas", "Feather-foot", or Kadicha." Kadicha are the indigenous shaman and healers. There are four different levels of spirituality in indigenous culture. There is everyday spirituality that everybody practises. Then, the healers and elders for each travelling mob. Then, the Kadicha, who look after several Mobs, are like priests. Then there is the Oruncha or High Kadicha, responsible for a whole area or language group. They are like an unquestioned Pope. They also live alone outside of any Mob but are free to visit any community that they need to. They are the keepers of the written language, and the message sticks by which they summon individuals or whole mobs or call council gatherings, celebrations, and invitations of corroborees. If the local elders cannot solve the problem, it is run up the ladder to the next level. Most things get solved internally very quickly. You do not want the solution to go to the Kadicha. The Kadichas are feared. They are used to scare miscreants and rebellious children, a little bit like bogeymen. If they are called in, they will solve the problem, but sometimes people will not like the solution to that problem. However, their decisions and actions are beyond questioning.

Because it is so powerful, in real terms, as well as in the hearts and minds of indigenous people, the practice of this spiritual tradition is still outlawed to this day. Our country pays lip service to equality; however, can indigenous people really be equal if their equivalent of Popes and priests are jailed for practising their indigenous traditions? Sure, not all of them are wise. They had a lot of tricks, magick and power, but even those fellows could make stupid judgment calls.

Donnie's dad, despite his training and abilities, was one of those who made some very bad personal decisions. Nevertheless, Donnie did get good training from his father. Training that many other Indigenous people have not had. Donnie is respected for his family lineage and his father's teachings, but mostly Donnie is respected because of his drive to share culture.

Donnie is passionate about sharing culture. He feels that many young indigenous men are trying to be young Afro-Americans instead of learning their own culture.

Donnie shares culture with us that is often kept from people outside his mob. He says;

> "I feel it is culturally essential to have Australian indigenous traditions remembered and shown as a testament to cultural pride and to highlight our dependence upon the land. We belong to the land. The land does not belong to us. My culture sharing helps people learn and understand this complex relationship. It shows that the land is alive and has a spirit and a soul, which was shared to give us life. We must stop our isolation from, and destruction of, the land, recognising that it has personality and that we can get to know it. Just like any family, the land needs us to survive, and we need the land for our immediate and individual survival. Culture sharing is a great common ground to provide a basis for acceptance of this fact and freedom from prejudice for the traditional peoples of the land. The focus of my work will be to use culture to help stop the rising death rate amongst the youth of the indigenous community. I feel if I can get the youth in our communities to focus on traditional art, music, dance and culture (rather than the Hollywood stereotype of African/American gangsters) that, this new cultural focus will give them a sense of pride, a reason to live and goals for the future. I have initiated a school program where I introduce traditional Australian indigenous cultural arts to young children. I have been a cultural liaison abroad to Japan and have had the honour of performing traditional didgeridoo music with the Sydney Philharmonic Orchestra. I have been acknowledged

within my community and by the Australian government as one of the best performers of traditional cultural dance and art alive in Australia today."

AUSTRALIAN INDIGENOUS SERVICE DURING WAR
Don't mention the war. Indigenous service and lack of recognition is a harrowing subject. For instance, Donnie's father was a highly decorated special serviceman in the army. He was sent on many secret and extremely dangerous missions because of his indigenous Kadicha skills.

After his service, Donnie's father was jailed for practising Kadicha for his people. It was very hard to keep him in prison. He lived up to the legend of Kadicha being able to walk through walls, and he went into hiding for decades, constantly moving. So Donnie was not close to his father, and he sees my husband Ken as a father figure. Donnie's father received no pension or thanks for his service, and he could not march with pride in Anzac Day parades. Donnie's dad had performed extreme services for this country. Yet, no recognition or help was ever given to him by the DVA. Donny's father was not alone in this, as the Department of Defence did not officially recognise the service of any indigenous person until 2023. The problem, according to the Department of Veteran Affairs website, is even though the Indigenous have served in every war in which Australia has been involved, The "Discriminatory enlistment standards.." made it hard for Indigenous people to receive a DVA entitlement, as they didn't officially exist! They were not officially allowed to join the defence forces, even though thousands did.

> "When the war began in 1914, the Defence Act 1903 (Cwlth) prevented Indigenous Australians from entering military service. Most recruiters rigidly stuck to the rule in their military recruiting handbook: "Aborigines and half-castes are not to be enlisted." This restriction is to be interpreted as applying to all coloured men. However, over the years of war, many Indigenous men were accepted into the AIF. Fewer and fewer Australians were willing to enlist as the war went on and casualty lists lengthened. ... Faced with rapidly declining numbers, the Australian Government began to relax the conditions for enlistment. First, it changed the physical requirements (age, height, chest measurement) to broaden eligibility. Then, it introduced legislation to accept enrolments from Indigenous Australians of mixed race. The new standard for enlistment in the 1917 Military Order 200(2) was: "Half-castes may be enlisted in the Australian Imperial Force provided that the examining Medical Officers are satisfied that one of the parents is

of European origin. NOTE — All previous instructions on this subject are cancelled." The relaxed standard made it easier for Indigenous Australians and people from other cultural groups to enlist in the AIF. They found some freedom in service.... they hoped for improved treatment and equality after the war.....We are working towards finding out more about the contributions of Indigenous men and women, but it remains a difficult task. .. This is why the full contribution of Australian Indigenous soldiers may never be completely understood. Thankfully, (some) Aboriginal and Torres Strait Islander peoples in World War I and later conflicts now (2023) receive the recognition they always deserved."

DVA (Department of Veterans Affairs) (2023), *Australian Indigenous service during World War I*, DVA Anzac Portal, accessed 24 January 2024, https://anzacportal.dva.gov.au/wars-and-missions/ww1/personnel/indigenous-service

POLITICAL MANIPULATION OF INDIGENOUS PEOPLE

There are some radical and extremist views put out into the public about the Indigenous by the propaganda machine of our government. They use woke sentimentality about indigenous discrimination to try to influence the result of referendums and local policy. The outcomes of these policies, in real terms, have no benefits to the indigenous community. Most indigenous would like the Australian government to stop touting them as the reason why they are trying to do things – most indigenous feel incredibly used by this process. The popular views that you hear in the media and from academia do not reflect the feelings or the problems of the larger indigenous population.

We have a history of government administrations being abused by a few indigenous who seize power and set themselves up as

Stone Circle Murwillumbah

Indigenous Wells

Fishtraps

Permanent Villages

Gympie Pyramid
'It is a crime under Australian law to destroy Aboriginal cultural heritage': Kabi Kabi Traditional Owners continue their fight to protect Djaki Kundu sacred site from highway expansion.

Relics at Gympie Site

Gympie Standing Stones carving

overlords. The indigenous derisively call these men "Big Fellas." Currently, one of these Big Fellas openly and famously channels money earmarked for Indigenous aid into mansions for his polygamous wives, aircraft to fly him in between these houses, real estate development deals, playing the stock markets and mining grants. None of this money is making its way through to the general population.

In 1993, I sent one of my university papers, highlighting the abuse of this system, to Alan Jones, who began a series of stories that brought down the first ATSIC (Aboriginal and Torres Strait Islander Commission.) ATSIC iterations operated for 15 years before being abolished by the Howard government in 2005. Some commentators called it *"..a failure mired in bureaucratic dysfunction."*

Nor do academic positions adopted by experts reflect indigenous dreaming or narrative. One of the main ones is that 'they were people in isolation for 40,000 years.' This is patently untrue. The Indigenous' own dreaming and narratives from various locations talk about the Indigenous over the millennia coming into contact with and absorbing many different races here in Australia.

The writings of Confucius indicate that Chinese mariners were visiting Australia between 592 and 553 BC. In Taipeh University, Taiwan, there are two ancient charts. Both date back 2000 years. One map depicts the south coast of New Guinea and the east coast of Australia as far south as Victoria and some of Tasmania's northern coastline. The other map, engraved upon a vase, shows Australia's scraggy but undeniable outline. And yet, we are still taught in our schools that Australian exploration only began 200 years ago with the arrival of Captain Cook. The Javanese certainly knew of Australia and still proudly display ancient maps depicting Australia as part of Indonesia.

The indigenous consider themselves a collective people. Not just because of the over 400 pre-existing language groups, each confined to its own very well-defined lands. An easy comparison in size and ratio are the nations of Europe. Each is an individual nation within one continent. All these different races may broadly be called European. There were wars and takeovers between these different indigenous nations, just as there have been in Europe and Africa for millennia. These different nations each document visitors from India, Asia, Polynesia, Egypt, The Middle East, and Scandinavian lands. Some dreaming specifically speaks of contact with people from beyond the stars. This dreaming includes extraterrestrial contact going back hundreds of years before the beginning of the UFO craze in the 1950s.

The elders know that Australia has not been isolated. And it has been inclusive for millennia. In the 1980s, I lived in Lismore and attended Tertiary education there. It was then called Lismore NRCAE. It had a sizeable indigenous contingent that meshed seamlessly with the rest of the students. So, it surprised my then-husband and I to be accosted by a group of militant young Indigenous as we were walking home late at night. They yelled at us, telling us to get out of their country and go back to where we came from. They were drunk, and we had been drinking. I realise this could get bad very quickly. So, I initially tried to talk my way out of this by telling them I was born here. The smell of this dirt runs through my blood. When they wouldn't listen to that, we tried explaining that my husband was 1/8th Bunjilung on his mother's side. But they were too drunk to listen to that.

An indigenous elder, a lecturer at the university, saw the disturbance and made his way towards us. He calmed the young fellas down and told them they had misunderstood his lecture. That the way to get the Whiteys out of Australia was not to kick them out but to breed them out. In the very near future, most people will have indigenous blood in their family, and their indigenous culture will absorb most Australians. He then acknowledged our heritage and spirituality in front of the group. "He is local blood, and I know his grandmother. And you, young lady, have more heart and dreaming than all these fellas put together." His saying this highlighted their ill manners and lack of indigenous etiquette as their prejudices had wanted to throw a person of their blood off their land. He had shamed them as they had behaved like uninitiated boys. They stared at the ground. The elder playfully grabbed the hair on the back of the ringleader's head to raise his head. He put his arm around him to lead him away, saying, "Isn't it more fun to make love than war."

That elder was right. My eldest son is 1/16th Bunjilung. Camping, fishing, BBQing (bush cooking), being part of the land, and of course, the dreaming are becoming increasingly part of our daily lives. So much so that when immigrants come from other countries, even though they are horrified at the primitiveness of these recreational practices, they begin to partake in them to become part of our community.

RESEARCH INTO INDIGENOUS PREHISTORY
Ancient Australian archaeology and indigenous prehistory are fascinating fields of study. We are only beginning to scratch the surface of what we know in these areas. Nearly every young graduating archaeologist I have spoken to is desperate to work overseas at famous dig sites. Yet many unexplored sites in Australia need preserving, cataloguing and studying in

a respectful and informed way. Very soon, archaeologists from the rest of the world will beg to come to Australia because of our exciting findings. Yet these sites here on our doorstep are not valued by Australians. I desperately encourage as many young people, indigenous and non-indigenous, as possible to become involved in this field of study. Understanding Indigenous pre-history will help us understand the pre-history of the entire world. The more we learn about it, the more we find the vital role Indigenous Australians have played in almost every early culture on this planet.

Scientists using current genetic testing point to a significant intake into Australia's population from Asia about 4000 years ago. Once in Australia, the ancestors of today's Indigenous communities remained almost completely isolated from the rest of the world's population until just a few thousand years ago, when they came into contact with some Asian populations, followed by European travellers in the 18th Century.

> "It's a really weird scenario," Willerslev said. "A few immigrants appear in different villages and communities around Australia. They change the way people speak and think; then they disappear, like ghosts. And people just carry on living in isolation the same way they always have. This may have happened for religious or cultural reasons that we can only speculate about. But in genetic terms, we have never seen anything like it before."

The paper, A Genomic History of Aboriginal Australia, is published in Nature. doi:10.1038/nature18299.

So-called "ghost populations" are groups of genetic signals that undoubtedly exist. We can see their history and results, yet no skeletons of the individuals who planted this genetic stream have been found for further study. It's not uncommon.

What the indigenous elder said in Lismore appears to have happened for millennia here in Australia.

Sometime later, I asked Donnie Didge about this, who is keen to establish the genetic link between the Tamil and the indigenous Australians. *"It's time for the academics to stop repeating the party lines so that they can get more funding and start telling the truth,"* he says. They were discussing this with indigenous elders, who were very much in agreement. They would rather this truth be made known rather than the academic propaganda that they have been a stagnant race for 40,000 years. The elders feel the Indigenous are being used as propaganda tools with this narrative.

It is often said that the only architecture of the Indigenous people was the travelling bush huts or humpies. However, this is not true. Many pre-colonial permanent stone and adobe structures from the Torres Strait to Bright in Victoria still exist. In Victoria, the indigenous people built homes for older people who could no longer travel along the Songlines. The complex fish traps that we find all around the Australian seaboard are some of the oldest human structures on this planet. The indigenous built an eel farm at Lake Conda. The indigenous people cultivated grains, and the Gunditjmara baked bread before the Egyptians learned how. The need for water accompanies agriculture, and today, we can find many remains of indigenous dams and wells. They made cloth out of both cultivated plants and animals. The Indigenous in Australia have been using boomerangs for tens of thousands of years. This complex form of asymmetrical single-wing lift is only beginning to be studied by aerospace experts as the most efficient

Well built timber & adobe cabins

-first contact-

Sydney Parkinson

Indigenous Australian wearing cloth garments

-first contact-

Image Detail

Sydney Parkinson

Image: Sydney Parkinson Descriptions of the well tended areas of coastline sound like gardens.:
"The Mountains or Hills are Checquered with woods and Lawns. Some of the Hills are wholy covered with flourishing Trees; others but thinly, and the few that are on them are small and the spots of Lawns"

"Two of the natives of New Holland advancing to combat."

-first contact-

Sydney Parkinson

way to produce aircraft. Thinking about it logically, assessing the number of artefacts needed for survival and for culture: rope, baskets, boomerangs, spears, shields, coolamon, canoes, nets, rope, shells, crystals, musical instruments, belts, garments, surplus grains, bread making equipment, ceremonial accoutrements, etc., the sheer volume of it requires a storage place. These were not disposable goods. They were not made and discarded at each camp. We know many of these were created and passed down through generations and cherished and stored at a place to come back to a permanent home. Indigenous villages and larger settlements are portrayed in several of the artworks created by early colonialists. Why have they slipped from our histories?

The remains of the astronomically aligned stone circle at Mullumbimby are also evidence of the indigenous people's complex cultural organisation and architectural abilities. The Gympie pyramid blocks were removed for road construction before they could be officially studied, which outraged both the indigenous and local residents. The Indigenous people of ancient times were known for their nationwide and overseas trade practices. It is surprising to note that tea-tree oil, which was widely used in the embalming process of the Egyptians, was sourced from far-flung sites, including Southeast Asia, thousands of miles away. This finding suggests that the embalming industry of Ancient Egypt played a crucial role in "early globalisation and global trade." says Stockhammer to Reuters' Will Dunham.

> "The Egyptians believed that preserving the dead was of utmost importance, as they thought the spiritual body would exist in an afterlife, quite similar to the living world." says The Australian Museum.

https://www.smithsonianmag.com/smart-news/the-surprising-substances-ancient-egyptians-used-to-mummify-the-dead-180981568/

Present in the embalmer's mix was gum from the tea trees, which grows only in tropical Southeast Asia or Australia.

> "This points to the fact that these resins were traded over very large distances and that Egyptian mummification was somehow a driver towards early globalisation and global trade," Stockhammer said.
>
> "Embalming was carried out in a well-organised, institutional way," said biochemist and study co-author Mahmoud Bahgat of the National Research Centre in Cairo.

https://www.scmp.com/yp/discover/news/global/article/3208856/ancient-egyptians-made-mummies-using-ingredients-far-southeast-asi

Elemis, also known as dammar or elemi, is a species of tree belonging to the plant family Burseraceae and native to Australia and Papua New Guinea. Its common name is Scrub Turpentine, and all three varieties of this tree are widely found in the northern regions of Australia. Although the name Elemi is not a Southeast Asian word, it is derived from an Arabic phrase that means 'above and below'. This phrase is an abbreviation of 'As above, so below' and tells us about the importance of Elemi to Arabic cultures and how they believed it acted on the emotional and spiritual planes.

Vast quantities of this oil would have been required to produce the hundreds of thousands of mummies exhumed in the late 1800s and exported back to England to be used as fire fuel. The bodies burned so efficiently because they had been soaked in oils, including tea tree oil. Combine this with evidence of the Gosford hieroglyphs and other Egyptian artefacts found in Queensland, and we get a picture of global export in trade dating back at least 3000 years.

We can trace indigenous DNA to Sri Lanka and India, meaning we know indigenous migrated offshore. We do not want to become like the Sri Lankan government, which is trying to remove all traces of indigenous Tamil pre-history to establish its authority.

The examination of the fascinating archaeology that remains today shows that Australia's indigenous culture was not limited to a stagnant, Stone Age nomadic lifestyle. Numerous large communities with permanent dwellings were arranged according to strict indigenous placement rules, similar to the principles of Feng Shui. Despite their vast distances, these communities connected to each other and nature, allowing them to come together for communal celebrations. Additionally, they had a writing system that unified the 400 nations across the continent and a Postal Service

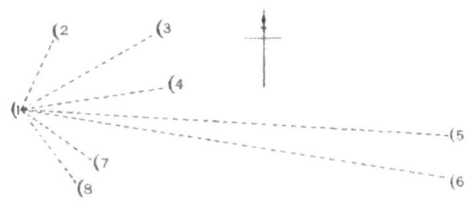

1. Man and wife.
2. Married son of 1. — 5 paces from 1.
3. Father and mother of 1. — 20 paces from 1.
4. Brother of 1 and wife. — 20 paces from 1.
5. Father and mother of the wife of 1. — 100 paces from 1.
6. Married son of 5. — The same distance.
7. The married brother of the mother of 1
8. The married sister of the father of 1.
} 10 paces each from 1.

If the sister of the wife of 1 had been present with her husband, they could have camped anywhere near, so long as not actually close to 1.

If there had been a married daughter of 1 there, her husband would have been in the same position as regards her mother as the wife of 5 was as to 1, and must have camped at a similar distance.

A *Brogan* who stands in the relation of brother to 1 could occupy a position suitable to that relation. Owing to the nature of the ground all the huts could face the sunrise, which is a favourite aspect.

Diagram From: Native Tribes of South-East Australia by Alfred William Howitt - 1904 - Chapter XII

https://en.wikisource.org/wiki/Native_Tribes_of_South-East_Australia

that could deliver messages anywhere in Australia. Unfortunately, there has been an attempt to ignore all traces of anything beyond the Stone Age nomadic culture, which is not an accurate representation of all of the indigenous culture in Australia. The lack of documentation of this history is a loss not only for the indigenous peoples of Australia but also for the whole world.

The Indigenous also feel that this 'unchanged-for-40,000-years' subtext portrays them as an undeveloped, stagnant race, and it is this, more than anything else, that allows the government to justify making 'progressive' decisions on their behalf. The wise old elders can see through the propaganda – because they know the truth.

The northern elders discuss the journey of the indigenous ancestors from India. The outward genetic similarities of the Northern Australian indigenous to the Tamil are there for all to see. Combine this with the northern indigenous stories of the long walk from the north to the south, and we get a bigger picture.

The Vedic culture also speaks about the exodus of those who sought to live a minimalist life after the Great Krukrashetra War, when the Vimana machines burnt the centre of the great Southland. In the ancient Hindu Vedas, there is a story called Drona Parva in the seventh book of the Mahabharata. The book describes Drona, a warrior appointed as leader of an army in the 18-day Kurukshetra War. This particular book provides some descriptions that sound eerily similar to the effects of a nuclear war:

> "We beheld in the sky what appeared to us to be a mass of scarlet clouds resembling the fierce flames of a blazing fire. From that mass, many blazing missiles flashed, and tremendous roars, like the noise of a thousand drums beaten at once. And from it fell many weapons winged with gold and thousands of thunderbolts, with loud explosions, and many hundreds of fiery wheels. "

Only eleven central warriors survive the war. After this, they renounced kingship and the materialistic life that had led to this massive destruction. They take their families and followers and travel south for a minimalist life in paradise. The timing of the writing of this account coincides with the genetic change in indigenous Australians.

This prompted a new round of genetic testing in 2013 of 130 north-end indigenous Australian nations, finding surprisingly uniform Tamil genetic markers. Theoretically, the Tasmanian indigenous may have been the original mainland inhabitants before the Tamil migration. However, they may have come across from New Zealand fly waves of Polynesian invaders. Like every nation on the planet, there has been a history of invasion, even before the whites arrived. I repeat these studies from a place of love. I have indigenous blood in my family, and my son, daughter-in-law, and granddaughter are of genetic indigenous heritage. Rather than live in denial, we must accept and love our history. And it is our history, not just indigenous history—scientifically proven true history – not false information where others try to manipulate us for their own ends.

Young Veddah Man From Sri Lanka

Young Australian Indigenous Northern Territory

Here are excerpts from an article from 14 January 2013 NATURE | NEWS

The Ancestors of Australia's Aboriginal Populations Were Not As Genetically Isolated From the Rest of the World as Once Thought.

The idea of an Indian link to ancient Australia is not altogether new. Dr Raghvendra Rao is a lead researcher from the Anthropological Survey of India and has been engaged in investigating contact between Indians and Australia's first peoples. Physical similarities with indigenous tribes in Southern India and Australian Aboriginal's were observed and studied in early anthropological studies as far back as the 1870s, researchers then suggested that links between ancient Indians and Australian Aboriginal tribes were based on measurements of the human body.

"This was one of the supports which we were building upon earlier studies in 1856 by Huxley, that there are morphological similarities between Indian and Australian Aboriginal tribes. This also was supported by Anthropometric evidence by Burt Shell. See any Australian Aboriginal photographs... and you see Central Dravidian tribes, you see the facial features are similar."

However, until a 90-year-old tuft of hair yielded the first complete genome of an Aboriginal Australian in 2011 – there was no real proof.

Genomes link Aboriginal Australians to Indians. Mingling of genes four millennia ago suggests continent was not isolated after all. Some aboriginal Australians can trace as much as 11% of their genomes to migrants who reached the island around 4,000 years ago from India, a study suggests. Along with their genes, the migrants brought different tool-making techniques and the ancestors of the dingo, researchers say.

This scenario is the result of a large genetic analysis outlined today in the Proceedings of the National Academy of Sciences." It contradicts a commonly held view that Australia had no contact with the rest of the world between the arrival of the first humans around 45,000 years ago and the coming of Europeans in the eighteenth century." says Mark Stoneking, a geneticist at the Max Planck Institute for Evolutionary Anthropology in Leipzig, Germany, who led the study.

Irina Pugach, a postdoctoral researcher in Stoneking's laboratory, discovered signs of the Indian migration by comparing genetic variation across the entire genomes of 344 individuals, including aboriginal Australians from the Northern Territory, highlanders from Papua New Guinea, several populations from Southeast Asian and India But Pugach found evidence of more recent genetic mixing, or gene flow, between the Indian and northern Australian populations taking place around 141 generations ago. She estimates that the Indians contributed nearly 10% to the Australian Aboriginal genomes. This gene flow could not have occurred during the initial wave of migration into Australia because it is absent from New Guinean and Mamanwa genomes. It is too uniformly spread across the northern Aboriginal genomes to have come from European colonists. The genetic mingling coincided with the arrival in Australia of microliths — small stone tools that formed the tips of weapons — and the first appearance in the fossil record of the dingo, which most closely resembles Indian dogs. All of these changes may be related to the same migration, the researchers say. "There have been very few genetic studies of Australians," Stoneking says, "and not anything like the dense, genome-wide study we carried out." A few smaller studies of mitochondrial DNA and the Y chromosome have hinted at recent gene flow between India and Australia, but a genome-wide study in 2010 missed it by not including any Indian populations, and a project that sequenced a full Aboriginal genome dismissed signs of gene flow from India as a spurious result.

Sheila van Holst Pellekaan, a geneticist at the University of New South Wales, Australia, and a co-author of the earlier genome-wide study, welcomes the latest research, She believes that the Aboriginals' vast genetic diversity suggests that multiple waves of migration could have occurred, but that new genes would not always have dispersed through the pre-existing peoples.

SBS -The Story Untold - The links between Australian Aboriginal and Indian tribes Published 21 March 2014 6:24pm -Updated 10 July 2019 10:52am By Kumud Merani

In a more recent study in 2022, researchers sequenced the complete genetic information of 83 Aboriginal Australians, as well as 25 Papuans from New Guinea, to produce a host of significant new findings about the origins of modern human populations. Their work is published alongside several other related papers in the journal Nature. The study, by an international team of academics, was carried out in close collaboration with elders and leaders from various Aboriginal Australian communities – some of whom are co-authors on the paper – as well as with various other organisations representing the participating groups. These include:
• Compelling evidence that Aboriginal Australians are descended directly from the first people to inhabit Australia – which is still the subject of periodic political dispute.
• Evidence of an uncharacterised – and perhaps unknown – early human species which interbred with anatomically modern humans as they migrated through Asia.
• Evidence that a mysterious dispersal from (Sri Lanka through) the northeastern part of Australia roughly 4,000 years ago contributed to the cultural links between Aboriginal groups today..".

The study's senior authors are from the University of Cambridge, the Wellcome Trust Sanger Institute, the Universities of Copenhagen, Bern and Griffith University Australia. Within Cambridge, members of the Leverhulme Centre for Evolutionary

Studies also contributed to the research, in particular by helping to place the genetic data which the team gathered in the field within the context of wider evidence about early human population and migration patterns.

For Dr Nitin Saksena, a Geneticist and Senior Research Fellow at the University of Sydney, the DNA evidence from a slew of new studies support the view of Indian migration to ancient Australia. "One the lineage of the mother the mitochondrial DNA that mother passes to children and that is quite clear… Then there is the study of Alan Red in 2010- this is done through the study of Y chromosome which is actually the paternal lineage, … both studies point out the relationship between the Australian Aboriginals, Papua New Guinea, Melanesians and also Indians."

When the Anthropological Survey of India sampled 966 samples of individuals from 26 different modern-day Indian tribes, they found a genetic marker that until recently had only been seen in Australian Aboriginals. Lead researcher Dr Raghvendra Rao, says maternal DNA passed down from linking mother to daughter over thousands of years reveals telltale genetic evidence of a deep link to Australian Aboriginals:
"Among them what we found was .. individuals shared a DNA linkage with the Australian Aboriginals that is M42. M42 is the DNA of Australian Aboriginals published earlier. These individuals came from Austro-Asiatic tribes from Eastern India and also Dravidian tribes from Central India."

The individuals with the 42 mitochondrial DNA marker is a prevalent genetic "sign-post" otherwise unique to Australian Aboriginals.

Geneticists now believe that the DNA record has solved another mystery of ancient Australia – the introduction of the Dingo and a sudden spread of sophisticated stone tools across the continent.

Dr Saksena thinks – it might have been the Indians who brought new technology and hunting dogs – that went on to become Australia's iconic wild canine, the dingo. "We currently know that the genetic link has been actually dated back through molecular dating to 4,300 years. And during that time we see actually the microlithic tools and the development of other tools for human survival which came into existence and also the fossils of the dingo were discovered at the same time in Australia."

But not all are convinced. Professor Lilley believes in his experience, working with tribal societies, a single human generation is more likely to be 15 or 20 years – bringing forward the arrival of the ancient Indians – by at the most - some 2,000 years. The genetic record now makes it seem certain that the Australian continent has witnessed the ebb and flow of waves of ancient migration and that in the centuries before the modern era families of people similar to tribes that still survive in southern India, came ashore on the beaches of northern Australia.

Bulu Imam, from the Indian National Trust for Art and Cultural Heritage at Hazaribagh in the Indian state of Jharkhand, has long believed in an Indian origin for the Dingo. Bula believes that the dingo is the direct descendant of the Indian pariah, which was taken by Indian hunters and gatherers to Australia 4,000 years ago. According to Bulu, the close resemblance of the Dingo to Indian Santal hounds, known as Pariahs – points to a common ancestor. His theory has been supported in the last decade with DNA evidence suggesting a common origin from a single Southern East Asian gene pool for most ancient dog breeds, including the dingo, the New Guinea Singing dog and the Pariah.

"Obviously, it is a direct importation of the Asian Pariah into the Australian continent at a fairly recent date because the DNA tests that have come from the Royal Institute of Technology in Stockholm show that the Indian Pariah is the same dog as the Indo-Polynesian breed and at a more recent dating has shown in China that the small Chinese wolf South of the Yangtze is the progenitor of the Asian Pariah.! DNA testing, which is conclusive evidence."

It's not the only physical evidence he believes links prehistoric India to Australia.

"The Cross in the circle – what you call the sun cross is first found in the world in the Kakadu National Park in Australia in Northern Arnhem land in 40,000 BC. Now, this is very interesting because the sun cross that is the circle with a cross in it is found all over the world now and in India, it is found in the Dravidian marriage rituals. In Jharkhand, it is a very common symbol in the marriage of these tribes. It is also found in the Metho Chalcolithic Rock Art in many parts of India including Hazaribagh.

"I believe the motif originated in Australia first by people who had the seen the Southern Star formation which is visible only in the Southern Hemisphere. This was 40,000 years ago... the cross in the circle, well, then I believe there could have been cultural migration of the symbols into India during several periods. It's not just 2,000 years ago that there was contact between India and Australia because we have to consider it in the context of the Anthropological and Archaeological evidence, that there was a proto Australoid migration out of Australia, which has come in parts to India."

Indians in Australia are also focussing on shared spiritual symbols Prem Mishra, a Hindu scholar with the Sri Mukti Gupteshwar Mandir Society in Sydney says Indian scriptures from the first and second millennium BC refer to Australia as the "Shaka Dweep" and describe the inhabitants as well... If you study the Shiv Shatra Rudra Samhita which is also part of the Shiv Puran,* there is also a very vivid description of Australia with various names like Astalid, Ashtalika. So quite a few names have been appearing in our ancient scriptures."

Prem Mishra interprets the scriptures to mean that Indians at that time knew about the great Southern continent – and considered Aboriginal Australians as part of their cultural world. "In the Hindu scriptures the Aborigines or the Adivasis of Australia have been very specifically defined as the Vedic (Hindu) people," he says.

"So the question comes why Vedic people? There is a very strong reason in that. In ancient times Vedic people used to worship three main aspects, that is Mother Earth and they used to worship the snake and also the fire. And the Aborigines of Australia are also worshippers of Mother Earth, the snake and in fact, the rainbow serpent theory is the mythical snake which links the mother Earth to heaven- that's their belief!" According to Vedic Hindi beliefs, the tail of the mythical snake is thought to protrude at the North pole and its head is wrapped around the Australian continent.

"That mythical snake that protects us from being destroyed on this planet," he says., "Its main part is positioned around Australia, so that's how its spirituality is described in our ancient scriptures. And that rainbow snake which is described as the Rainbow Serpent is worshipped by Aborigines as well." Prem Mishra also believes that the great Australian landmark – Uluru - is referred to in ancient scriptures as the "Ganapati Shila". Ganesha or Ganapati is the Elephant-headed God whom Hindus worship as the remover of all obstacles. Viewed at a certain angle he says Uluru looks like a mighty elephant at rest. He also points out that the ancient Indian word "Uru" means a high or important place."

But if Australia has left its mark on India - are there traces of India in the cultures and symbols of Australia? Aboriginal Australian and Archaeologist, Mark Dugay-Grist is from Western Victoria. He says Dreamtime stories and other oral traditions of the Aboriginal communities do tell tales of people from faraway lands coming to their country. "We have stories that have people coming from the stars, we have stories of people coming from overseas on ships. So, yes, we do have stories... where people have come from overseas..."
Ku Ku Kurri dances of Australia! Well, we have the Koori dances here too, they are done the same way, you put your arm around the companion's waist and then people get into a line and they jump and sing around the fire."

Similarities With Language
It's not just in stories - Bulu Imam, at the Indian National Trust for Art and Cultural Heritage, believes the ancient Indians have left footprints in indigenous Australian languages. "I have done a lot of study on the comparison of languages and I'm not surprised that hundreds and hundreds of root words are more or less exactly the same... unchanged!"

Using Margaret Sharpe's Macquarie – "Aboriginal words" Bulu has documented many similar words in the Bundjalung language spoken in the Northern Rivers area of NSW and the language of

the Birhors, which is spoken by a little-known jungle tribe of Chota Nagpur in India. For example:
The word "naked" in Birhori is "nunga" – it's the same in Bundjulung.
The word for "woman" is "Kuri" in both languages.
Topsy-turvey also exactly the same – "Palti".
Even basic vocabulary is the same. "Father" in Bundjalung is "Baban" and in Birhori it is "Baba".
The word "new" in both languages is 'Nia', the word "good" is 'bugal"
Bulu believes that these words could share a common origin.
Bulu Imam, at the Indian National Trust for Art and Cultural Heritage, believes that now the genetic and historic connections have been made – the link between India and Australia's indigenous cultures will flourish.

About 90% of Aboriginal communities today speak languages belonging to the "Pama-Nyungan" linguistic family. ... Language experts are adamant that Pama-Nyungan languages are much younger, dating back 4,000 years, and coinciding with the appearance of new stone technologies in the archaeological record.

Please check out the Indigenous dictionary at the end of this book for your chance to learn a few Indigenous words.

POPULATION "Y"

In 2015, two geneticists named Tábita Hünemeier and Marcos Araújo Castro e Silva discovered "Population Y." This discovery was made after studying the DNA of over 200 living and ancient individuals from two Indigenous Amazonian groups, the Karitiana and Suruí. The research revealed that these groups have Australian indigenous ancestry. The Y signal, a set of genetic markers, was found in many individuals, and it is named after the Brazilian Tupi word for "ancestor," ypikuéra. Some scientists believe the Y signal was present in some of the earliest South American migrants. In contrast, others think the signal was introduced by a later migration of people related to present-day Australasians. These people share a genetic connection with native Australians and Melanesians.

In 2021, Hünemeier tested 383 modern individuals across South America, including dozens of newly genotyped individuals living in the Brazilian

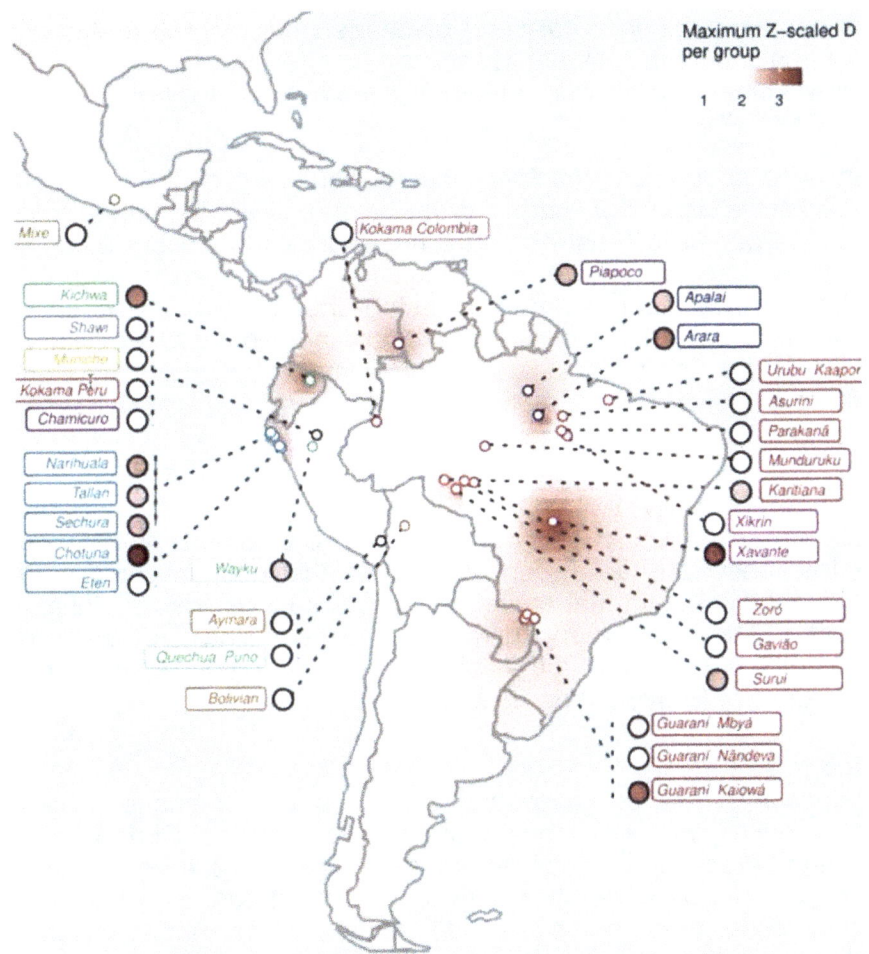

Amazon and central plateau. The researchers collaborated with Indigenous people, historians, anthropologists, and geneticists in their work,

> "…..to assure the results would be transferred in the best way to the Indigenous communities."

Scientists have recently discovered the Y signal in groups outside the Amazon region. This genetic signal of Australasian ancestry was identified in the Xavánte people who live on the Brazilian plateau and

The above image shows the density of the "Y Population' genetic signal in South America.

in the Chotuna people of Peru, descended from the Mochica civilisation that occupied the country's coast between 100 C.E. and 800 C.E. This

signal has been found in far-flung places, such as Vietnam, Japan, and Siberia, making it a fascinating discovery.
https://www.science.org/content/article/earliest-south-american-migrants-had-australian-melanesian-ancestry

It has been suggested that there was a significant migration of people from Australia to other parts of the world. This indicates that the indigenous people of Australia were not 'isolated' for over 40,000 years but rather had extensive contact with both nearby and distant populations. This fact has been well-established for over a decade. If this information were widely publicised, modern indigenous Australians could take great pride in their ancestors' achievements as great explorers and migrators. It is truly an impressive feat for any race.

RESPECT FOR BUNYIPS, YOWIES & MI MI
Indigenous Australians do not consider these creatures simply myths and fairytales. They are an essential part of their culture and heritage. Traditional beliefs hold that these are real spiritual beings that inhabit the landscape. There are many dreaming stories telling of friending and placating these beings. It is the height of I'll manners to scoff at or make fun of stories of Bunyips. Yowies and Mi Mi.

Yowies
Many locals have reported yowie encounters in the hinterland of the Gold Coast. Yowies are like the Australian version of Bigfoot or The Abominable Snowman. These reports date back to the early first settlers. One historical police report claims a man captured a juvenile Yowie, which he locked in his outhouse, until it broke out, causing devastation to their farm and local community. The exciting thing about this report is that there is no hint of disbelief like the existence of Yowies was taken as a given.

The people I have spoken to who have had encounters described them as large, ape-like, hairy and smelly. They walk perfectly erect, between 7 to 9 feet tall (2 ½ - 3 metres). The ones who have seen their faces say the face is very human, and the eyes are very bright and intelligent. They can crash through thick rainforests at high speed, though they seldom chase after humans. Yet many have described being roared at and scared by them.

The highly regarded Australian naturalist David Fleay encountered them. David Fleay was the first person to breed a platypus in captivity. He outlined the protocols for breeding wedge-tail eagles and reintroducing them into the wild. He was one of the first naturalists in the '60s and '70s to publish papers on preserving endangered species from extinction. He had won scientific awards worldwide. He was highly regarded and often quoted in academic circles around the world. Until he published his paper on his encounters with the Yowies who lived in the remote rural areas of his large fauna sanctuary in Tallebudgera Valley. The academic community turned their back on him. However, the paper that he published is compelling. He believed that the Yowies were dying out and that immediate action had to be taken to preserve the ingress of humanity into their remote habitat.

My 168-acre retreat centre, Shambhallah, was near David Fleay's centre. I have heard gigantic creatures crashing through the thick rainforest, accompanied by a terrible smell. Yet, I have never seen them personally. I believe the closest I came was on an early morning bush walk climbing 'The Pinnacle' in remote northern New South Wales. My husband and I were being very quiet. It became so quiet; it was like the whole world had gone away, as sometimes happens when you are alone in a very, very thick fog. We became aware we were being followed by something substantial, making unusual, grunting-growling sounds. The sound was getting louder as it was getting closer and closer. It did not get close enough for us to have a good look at it. Nor did we want it to. It crashed away through the thick rainforest when it heard other climbers noisily approaching along the path from the other direction. We could tell it was very tall as it sped away through the trees.

Many locals do claim to have seen them. They are usually terrified when they recount details. The people I have spoken to are not the kind to give into flights of fantasy. For instance, my father's boss encountered one while driving towards the Springbrook Mountain tick-gates. He said he saw what he initially thought was an injured person hunched over beside the road. He stopped and opened his door to ask them if they were okay. When spoken to, the creature stood up and glared at him. It was over 7 feet tall. He said he knew this because the truck he was driving had a 6-foot clearance, and the creature was standing down in the gutter at the side of the road. He could only see its eyes, not the top of its head. It then roared at him and ran into the bush. My father's boss was a massive, tough, sceptical man, but he was so scared that he wet himself. He described the lingering smell of the creature as being so intense that he also vomited. Soon after, he sold his business's freehold land for redevelopment and returned to England.

The indigenous say that the Yowie's are the change bringers. When they are seen, or their presence is felt, significant changes happen in an individual's life and the lives of the whole community around them. The indigenous word "Yowie" means "spirit being." The indigenous believe that Yowies are part spirit, part physical. That they are from another place and that they can move between worlds. That they are from another dimension parallel to our own yet apart. Only certain people can see them. They can appear to bring justice or to protect. Sometimes, Yowies allow themselves to be seen when a person needs to change their direction in life. The indigenous consider Yowies to be sacred and potentially dangerous and need to be treated with great respect.

Several credible trail cam images have surfaced in recent years.

Bunyips

Bunyips are different to Yowies. Bunyips are purely spirit. A water spirit that lives in waterholes. They can emerge and move in the physical world, given the correct circumstances. Some people can see them, but they are not physical. They guard the sacred waterholes, protecting the reincarnation of the future generations.

I have personally had an experience with a bunyip at my Shambhallah retreat. We had 168 acres in Tallebudgera Valley, considered remote and rural in its day. We had three water holes. One large water hole at the front of the property had a gentle swimming pool with a sudden drop-off. During the day, it was frequented by children who would swing from homemade rope swings in the trees to plunge into its depths.

Not long after we took possession of the property, I put my children to bed and decided to take some night air and quietly meditate by the waterhole. It was a moonlit night and very warm, pleasant and peaceful. I sat down, opened my third eye and started meditating. With my eyes closed, I could tell the night was getting brighter and thought the moon had come out from behind the clouds. When I opened my eyes, the moon still could not be seen above the trees. Instead, the source of light was coming from under the water. Something was shining in the deepest depths of the drop-off. I was fascinated. I had seen fireflies and glowing mushrooms on the property. I had seen strange lights in the sky. Yet, I had never seen anything like this before or since. I leant over the waterhole, expecting to see some sort of glowing fish coming to the surface. Then I realised it was too large and bright to be any sort of fish. The light kept growing brighter and was moving towards the surface. I'm never afraid of things in the bush, but a wave of fear washed over me. All the hair on my body stood on end, and I turned and ran, without thinking, back towards the house.

Sometime later, I was very privileged to speak about this event with Donnie Didge, an indigenous elder who often comes to share culture with us at our "On Country" retreats.

Donnie told me that the Bunyips still live in many deep, sacred waterholes. He said that what I had seen was very typical Bunyip behaviour. He felt it was only letting me know it was there. Although he said there are many dreaming stories of Bunyips rising to the surface and stealing women and taking them back to their watery realm. He said that if they like you, they can protect you and the people around the area. Donny advised me to get on the Bunyip's good side by leaving him regular offerings of honey – which I did!

Min Min Lights
These are mischievous spirits in nature. They love to play tricks on humans or scare them. Myths abound of fairy lights in the forest, getting people hopelessly lost. In Australia, this is called The Min Min Light, and we are taught from early childhood never to follow the Min Min. The Min

Min light is a phenomenon reported from as far south as Brewarrina in western New South Wales to as far north as Boulia in northern Queensland. It takes its name from the small township of Min Min, located between the outback towns of Boulia and Winton, where the light was first reported by a local stockman in 1918.

> "The Min Min light seems to have magical qualities, sometimes following observers, even as they speed away in vehicles, while at other times seeming to retreat shyly. Even hardened Outback observers can break down when they are unable to interpret the unusual optical properties of the light in their own terms, past experiences" says Professor Pettigrew, who is the Director of UQ's Vision, Touch and Hearing Research Centre,

He used his skills in the vision sciences combined with extensive first-hand experience of the Diamantina region of Western Queensland at night to postulate on the Min Min. While studying the nocturnal letter-winged kite in the region, he encountered the phenomenon. He feels it may be a form of the Fata Morgana.

> "Named after the Morgan fairy, who was reputed to be able to conjure cities on the surface of the sea ice, the Fata Morgana is a real physical phenomenon, caused by a temperature inversion. A cold, dense layer of air carries light far over the horizon to a distant observer without the usual dissipation and radiation, to produce a vivid mirage that baffles and enchants...."

Stories about the lights are in Aboriginal myths pre-dating western settlement. Indigenous Australians say that the number of sightings has increased since the arrival of Europeans. The lights sometimes follow or approach people or cars and disappear when shot at, only to reappear later. Similar to stories by the Inuit about the Aurora Borealis, local legends say that anyone who follows the lights will never return. Despite intense interest in the Min Min, they had never been explained satisfactorily.

The MiMi

The indigenous seldom mention the MiMi as it is thought to bring bad luck. When they do talk about the indigenous fairy folk, "MiMi" is their word for the little troublemakers. They are described as being very black in appearance. They dart around, hiding in the lonely bush, playing tricks on humans and animals, then hiding and watching the resultant chaos at a safe distance. They can only be seen out of the corner of their eye. They antagonise people who introduce foreign garden plants or litter or invoke European fairies and imps without asking their permission. The last thing you need on your land is a fairy war. They like smashing garden statues, especially gnomes. They can be pacified by asking their permission before you plant anything and by leaving them small offerings of honey and small amounts of alcohol around your garden.

Far-right, behind the children, has been identified as a MiMi, an indigenous trickster fairy, rarely seen and even less often photographed.

I was gifted this photo by a local indigenous Aunty from Loganholm Queensland. She wishes to remain anonymous. I have her permission to publish as she has also posted it on Facebook. Yet even whilst trying to add this photo it kept jumping all over the page!

Totems

A totem is a spirit being, sacred object, or symbol of a tribe, clan, family or individual. The Australian Indigenous traditions connect with all life as equally sacred. Many mobs allocate three animal totems to each person: their birth totem, marriage totem and hidden transformation totem. The birth and marriage totems are generally allocated at birth. The hidden totem may be allocated at any time during their life. Often, the totem animal will choose an individual by being repeatedly significant in their life. The totem is there to teach, protect, or both. Any connection felt with an animal, bird, fish, insect or mythical animal is significant. The connection may be a totem of great value. The indigenous believe the animal totems to be part of their spirit. As such, they will NEVER eat their totem animal. Animal totems can be teachers, protectors and comforters. If you are attracted to an animal, bird, fish, insect or mythical animal, listen for messages from that being. There are qualities in that animal that you may need in your life.

Birth Totems

The birth and marriage totems are the same for the indigenous, but not always. There may be a time with growth and change when the birth totem moves in the background, and another totem is drawn forward. Another animal totem may be drawn in if an individual's life changes drastically by chance or choice.

Marriage Totems

The easiest way to keep track of 1st cousins and intertribal blood relationships is with birth totems. They are allocated to prevent intermarriage of closely related people. It may take some time for the elders to calculate who can have children with whom. Based on the animal totems, it is easier to know who the likely candidates of breeding age are within the local and the surrounding mobs. Sex was different. Sex was fun and easy, but marriage was serious. Do you feel that you have been looking for another of your kind? That you are a lone surviving member of a species on the verge of extinction. Then you find another like you. This is a marriage totem—the same type of person as you but in the body of the opposite sex. Indigenous Australian traditions say that it is very hard to fall pregnant if you and your partner do not share the correct marriage totem.

YENDAKARANGU TOTEMS

Class	Totems	Marries with
Kararu	Cloud	Wadnamura
	Crow	Wadnamura and Eagle-hawk.
	Red ochre	Cormorant and *Eagle-hawk*.
	Rat	Cormorant and Bull-frog.
	Wallaby	Iguana and *Lizard*.
	Emu	Eagle-hawk and *Bull-frog*.
	Musk duck	Eagle-hawk and *Dog*.
	Snake	Wadnamura.
Matteri	Eagle-hawk	Red ochre, Musk duck, and *Crow*.
	Cormorant	Rat and Red ochre.
	Iguana	Wallaby.
	Dog	Musk duck.
	Wadnamura	Snake, Cloud, Crow.
	Mulga tree	Emu.
	Bull-frog.	Rat.
	Lizard	Wallaby.

Totems and Your Dreams

A totem can spontaneously connect in dreams and meditations. It can teach the individual about themselves. A totem can give courage and wisdom. A totem brings the subconscious to the conscious. The Indigenous pay attention to their dreams. Totems often speak in dreams.

THE KOOKABURRA TOTEM

A kookaburra saved my life.

I'm Ken Wills, and the kookaburra is my totem.
They talk to me and laugh at my jokes.
I like them, and they like me.

I can do a fair imitation of their call. Indigenous legends say that I should not do this. Anyone learning a new language picks up swear words as an introduction, especially if they come into contact with someone in a pub or club. They think it is hilarious watching you try to mimic their language whilst swearing at the top of your voice in a crowded bar, especially if the bar is full of people who know what you are trying to say. This is how I learned to talk Kookaburra; I think the joke is on me.

Kookaburra Image Copyright Ken Wills 2011

There are tales of how the kookaburras punish children who mimic them. Some tales say the kookaburras won't let the sun rise or prevent rains falling if they are offended by an impersonator. My kookaburras make it rain when I laugh at them. If I have a few drinks at a get-together and then call to them, they answer by making the skies open up and the water come forth all over everyone. This trick, though impressive, does not help my popularity at parties.

Shé, my partner, threatened me with all sorts of terrible things if I were to call to my

Kookaburras during the "On Country" event at Dunns Swamp. It was very tempting. There was a family of five kookaburras watching us all weekend. Each time I sighted them I had to fight the urge to call to them. They were trying to tease me into it. They kept calling to me. Bating me, but I didn't take the bait.

The Kookaburras were everywhere I went that weekend, just watching and waiting, tempting me to call in the storms to make all the tents fill up with water and then blow away... But I was good. I restrained myself... well... until the very last moment. I called to them as we were packing up to leave. The skies became overcast, and by the evening, it started to spit. It grew gradually heavier through the night. It rained and rained and rained. It rained up and down the eastern seaboard for a week, severely flooding northern NSW. (Oops!...)

I respect my totems. I would never harm them. They are adaptable hunters. Like me, they will hunt on land, but they love fishing. They can catch fish that are greater than their body weight. I love big game fishing too.

My friend Kevin Kelly, a good, down-to-earth lad of Irish descent and brilliant musician who plays the Irish Drum called the bodhran, was with us at Dunn's Swamp. In his hands, this instrument becomes more than a drum; it speaks all languages and breaks all cultural barriers; even the gods listen when he plays. The Kookaburras over the weekend were no different; every time he held a drumming circle or class, the Kookaburras would kick in from their ringside seats in the trees around the campsite. During the classes, he would have to wait a minute or two before he spoke to give us the next part of the lesson, as his voice could not be heard over the chorus of his backup singers in the trees above. - It is hard to get good help.

This is so kookaburra. They are such tricksters with a great sense of fun who love human company and want to interact. Their call can often be the herald of spirit in the area.

Perhaps the kookaburras were trying to tell us they weren't the only ones interacting. Kevin did a lot of drumming in a large cave next to the campsite over the four days we were there. The Elders had told me this cave was used as a lookout post in earlier times. Usually, one male person would keep watch from there at all times. White settlers out to hunt the local indigenous people could be spotted from these lookout posts scattered all through the surrounding bush. During the weekend, several people came to me and told me that during the evening, whilst

Kevin had been drumming, they had seen someone looking out at our campsite from that spot. They all described the same thing: a black male with white hair and beard standing at the entrance to the cave. Strangely, he did not look upset or guarded; they all told me he was smiling. So it appears that Kevin Kelly has a fan in the spirit world too.

When you identify with an animal and realise it is your totem, you look after it, and it looks after you in the same way that the watcher at the cave looked out for his people.

Once, when driving up north to do a psychic fair, we travelled through very heavy traffic in convoy with many army vehicles on the road. Some sort of army games. This was very unusual as these roads tend to be sparsely trafficked. Instead, there were a lot of large army semi-trailers carrying tanks and trucks.

We had been making good time. We had progressively overtaken much of this endless column. Just as we were overtaking one of these trucks near the head of the column, a Kookaburra flew into my car.

The kookaburra wasn't trying to cut across my path. It did something I have never seen another bird do. It flew up the main highway straight towards my jeep. It must have seen me but did not swerve; it just kept flying directly for me like a little feathered guided missile. I braked and tried to slow down, yet it still hit hard. It made impact with the windscreen just in front of my face. It went limp, and the slip-stream brushed it off my car to the left like a fallen leaf; Woosh. Gone! There was no blood, but it could not have survived. I had to pull over to search for it immediately. Even though we would lose our opportunity to move ahead and away from the column of army vehicles. I felt I had to go back and look for the body of my little mate. He was my totem and, therefore, family. I couldn't just leave him there.

I searched the left-hand side of the road for a kilometre from the point of impact. Nothing. So I searched the right-hand side, but nothing was there either. It couldn't have just vanished. So, after searching for a long enough time for all the army vehicles to overtake us again, I eventually assumed that my little mate had survived and had flown off somewhere to recover from a massive headache.

I guess I had spent 30 minutes looking for the bird to no avail. As I stepped back into my jeep, there was a loud explosion about ten kilometres further up the highway. I looked up to see a giant mushroom cloud rising into the air; some lesser blasts followed this.

It had come to a standstill when we caught up to the end of the army column. We found out that an army trailer carrying a tank near the head of the line had crashed head-on into a semi-trailer coming the other way. The explosions we had heard were the live ammunition the tank was carrying. If we had continued, we would have been very near this explosion when it occurred. Could it have been the truck I was overtaking when the kookaburra dived at my screen? We will never know for sure. We waited for a while, not knowing the extent of the accident. Eventually, one of the army blokes in a truck near us radioed the front of the column. He blanched and started running up the line. He shouted back to us that this mess would not be cleared up for hours. So, I faced the car the opposite way to my destination and drove back up through the hills and around the accident. It was a three-hour detour.

The early morning news reported that the highway was closed till 3 am the next morning. There had been fatalities. The fire and explosions had melted the tar off the road, and a specialist emergency road crew was needed to reconstruct the main highway just north of Rockhampton urgently. We had been lucky not to have been caught up in this tragedy.

Was my little mate risking his own life in an attempt to try and warn me of the impending danger? I would like to think so. This is what I mean about totems looking after you. They do if you will listen.

Luck, coincidence, Maybe. Maybe not. Call it what you will, but I, for one, will be looking for those signs from my laughing mates in the future. I think we all see them. Yet, we dismiss them too casually without fully analysing what our totems are trying to tell us.

Out totems are our connection with nature to let us know what is best for us, physically mentally and spiritually. Take a moment to listen to those signs. Go with your gut feeling, not what your heart or brain tells you.

That is the end of my kookaburra tale. I will let you be the judge.....

© Copyright Ken Wills Sunday, December 18, 2011, Gold Coast Australia

THE BUTTERFLY TOTEM

Imagine how it feels to come loose in the stream of time.

It gives life a heady seasickness. You float and roll through existence like a butterfly tossed on the breeze. Foreseeing and knowing the moments of your great joys and sorrows can make the journey through life perfunctory. Pretending not to see doesn't work. There are few surprises. Surprises happen way before they occur, and that pleasant slap loses its joyful sting. Alternative futures are previewed mid-flight.

You would think that would make it easy to always sail towards personal joy. However, already knowing the cost, the choice is often a direction that nobody expects or understands but you. That one erratic flap of the butterfly's wing can have a greater beneficial effect on so many people it outweighs the choice to steer directly towards your personal happiness or the happiness of those near and dear to you.

Shé Butterfly Whispering - © Ken wills 11th Jan 2007

Imagine seeing all the outcomes, all the results of all the possible choices before they occur. The euphemism "The Butterfly Effect" takes on a new and very personal meaning. The alternative possibilities of one's death become a matter of guilt. Should I choose the peaceful one that inspires loss and love in my nearest and dearest or the violent one that inspires outrage and significant change? Wrestling at night with selfish choices, knowing the far-reaching consequences can make one dark. However, the lucky ones see the alternative to the darkness. Grasping the incredible lightness of being, they choose the fleeting buoyant dance, like Dionysus, the god of relief from suffering, that leaves catharsis and wonder in its wake.

THE SWAMP

Knowing that your own extinction could be a good thing is something many would resist and find too disturbing to live with. Many who have this gift or curse do lose their minds, and we ignore them daily when we see them sitting muttering on street corners with tin cups in their hands. These lost souls are a radio between stations picking up echoes from the future and the past. Their wings have been crushed, so they just sit there and fade.

Dunn's Swamp View by © Ken Wills 2006

It gets to me sometimes. I can't always do the Dionysian dance with my mind. Sometimes I feel awful. It shows. Sometimes, it looks like my body has moved forward in the stream of time. Sometimes, I look much older than my 60 years. I start to fade. Yet, I can't just sit there like that. So, I run away. I hide in nature's expanded view of existence.

When I was in one of my runaway moods, a friend invited me to a place called Dunn's Swamp in The Blue Mountains Wollemi National Park.

"A swamp? Sure! Why not!" I thought, "This place will not see me at my best. A swamp might be appropriate."

Yet, it was not what the name implied. It was beautiful. Vast vistas are like a mini Katherine Gorge with bright-coloured ocha cliffs, natural pagoda rock outcrops, new stalactite formations, and deep clean water. The purest water. This place breaks all the rules. It is the opposite of the implication of dank degeneration that the name implies. Everything that the environmentalists say must happen is not happening there. Because of human actions, extinction is in reverse. Though academic experts oppose 'artificial water management,' this place proves that common sense human intervention can improve things.

A dam was built 70 years ago by the local Kandos Cement Works to ensure water supply to their business during drought. The tired, dry land was waiting for this and responded by multiplying the profusion of life. Species are not dying out; they are coming back. Contrary to what is claimed by the green lobbyists, this new water reservoir did not destroy the native flora and fauna. Instead, species long thought extinct are being rediscovered here. Once forgotten food for dinosaurs, the Wollemi Pine is now feeding other returning species. The seeds sat dormant in the quiet earth, patiently waiting for a drink. The yellow-spotted bell frog, thought to have been extinct for 40 years, has been rediscovered in this pristine wilderness. Frogs will bury themselves in the earth, dehydrate, and enter extended periods of hibernation, waiting for water to return. They did when it did. Endangered birds, including lyrebirds, kingfishers, swamp harriers, peregrine falcons, brush stone-curlews, bitterns, grass birds, regent honeyeaters, square-tailed kites, plus scarlet-chested, swift, turquoise and king parrots all flourish here. Woylies, extinct everywhere except for one other place, have recently been sited here. Numbats that have been extinct in New South Wales for over 100 years have been seen here. In the 60-foot deep water, platypus, rare eels, giant Murry cod and lungfish abound.

This is beyond extinction. There is regeneration. It regenerates me. It is an amazing place. The energy is palpable.

I knew it would regenerate others. I knew I would have to share this with a select few who would understand, those who would feel connected with the land.

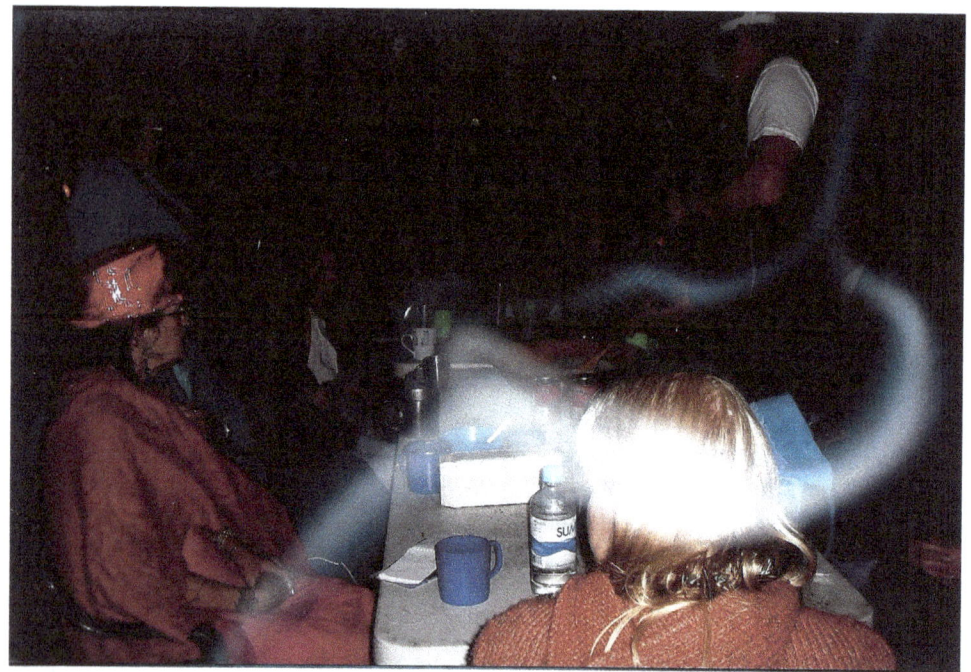

SPIRIT GUIDES

When we did come back, we came back with 40 deeply spiritual people. This included a dear friend of mine from the United States. Oberon Zell Ravenheart is a living wizard, author, artist, sculptor, inventor, crypto, zoologist, and father of the worldwide neopagan movement. A remarkable man. My friend, who had initially suggested that I visit this location, arranged for us all to meet the local elders of the Wiradgery. They welcomed us On Country. They accepted gifts from us. They exchanged culture.

While we were there, remarkable things happened. Native fauna approached individuals within the group without fear. We were able to view very ancient Australian cave paintings. The women visited an Indigenous birthing cave hidden in the middle of the lake.

The energy was high. The camaraderie was strong. These photos were taken by Georgina Woodberry on the last day of our Australian Indigenous "On Country" retreat at Dunns Swamp. The local elders had been there that day and given us their blessing. We had just participated in a kava ceremony (promoted as an alternative to alcohol amongst the indigenous people) and

thanked those people who helped us. In the ceremony, we invited the local keepers of this sacred place in spirit to be present with us in our final circle. As we did this, Ken called out and pointed to a rock ledge overlooking where we were camped.

A visible silhouette of an indigenous warrior standing on one leg, watching us, is seen by everyone. From these photos, we can see plenty of spirit with us at the campsite, too, unseen by our physical eyes but captured on film. Spirit swirls around Ken Wills in this first photo from the On Country Retreat as he performs the Kava Ceremony.

Spirit hands manifesting in photos of me has been a recurring theme since childhood. Here is one manifesting above my head, along with the outline of my guide, in the indigenous red and black colours.

The Gypsy woman standing in front of me, getting a round of applause, was our cook; her surname was Fyre. No wonder she was enveloped in red light.

This was taken on the same night. Seen here is Oberon Zell-Ravenheart. We had just placed candles with our wishes onto a metal tray near the campfire. We dedicated these to the spirits of the indigenous who had died here during the massacres. We asked Oberon to thank the traditional guardians and to close the event for us by releasing the spirit we had invoked. We also asked him to take goodwill from us back to the US with him. Looks like the spirits were hopping on board for the trip overseas.

GHOSTS
A pretty white butterfly marked in black and yellow has been rediscovered here, too. The Caper White (Belenois java teutonica) is sometimes called the Australian ghost butterfly or Casper by children, after the comic-book friendly-ghost. Spirit connections are often better sensed by children. This is an appropriate nickname for a pale symbol of regeneration that is here one minute and gone the next. The caper white is one of the most common butterfly species in Queensland and South Australia. It is a strong flyer, able to travel a 3000-kilometre round trip as it can only breed on caper trees native to Queensland, from which it gets its name. Why they should fly south to colder areas where their caterpillar food plants do not exist is unknown. In some years, enormous numbers fly west through inland Queensland, from Townsville to Toowoomba, heading south over the inland border corner for the town of Marion in the Flinders Rangers of South Australia. This white ghost-like invasion delights everyone and provides food for many thousands of birds along the way. The caper white butterfly has not been seen in living memory in The Blue Mountains, yet they were everywhere whilst I was there.

I was feeling terrible after an episode of betrayal by two friends. By her childish actions, one supposed friend had severed a 20-year friendship and working relationship I had with another friend. She had also cost me a lot of money by pulling out, at the last minute, of the last few public appearances in her Australian tour that we had planned and advertised for the previous ten months.

It was the end of a phase of my life. I let it affect my health, and I developed severe allergic hay fever. The late spring pollen was trying to make love to my nose and would not take No! for an answer. I felt raped by my friends and nature. I had seen the betrayal coming and had tried to appeal to their better nature and change its course towards something where we all would win. Nevertheless, they were functioning from the lower, selfish side. This was a moment of a nexus of change for me. This is one of those moments where I could choose the future that would lead to a peaceful death. Were people worth the effort, the unpleasantness and the inconvenience? I felt like walking away from everything and everyone, so I went to the swamp for two weeks and did just that. However, I was not alone.

Everywhere around me, these white, wistful beings played with nature. They extended their long proboscises into the open womb of flowers

Caper White On melaleuca Flower Dunn's Swamp © Ken Wills 27th November 2010

without resistance. They drained the sweet nectar of life from each waiting blossom and passed on to the next one, as light and carefree as you please. The things I found irritating were nourishing them and causing fertility and regeneration for each bloom they loved and left. The butterflies were holding up the universal billboard to me whilst each sneeze made me feel that if I did not read the sign, I would be hit over the head with it again and again until I listened.

So, I stopped hiding, and I refused to be defeated. It was not my time. If I gave up now, I would get temporary peace, but would I be able to sleep knowing that I walked away from so many who needed me and would need me in the future? No! Therefore, I continued with my contractual migration down to Melbourne, made more money, and succeeded more than I would have if my friends were still working with me. I regenerated and reinvented myself. The stress transformed my work into something even more beautiful. Then, I flitted back to Queensland.

Six months later, my partner Ken Wills and I were reviewing his beautiful photos of this transformative trip. I looked at his fantastic butterfly photos and felt something was wrong. I got the strongest, strangest feeling that those should not be there. I mentioned it to Ken, and he said that a local man, Colin, had said that he had not seen them before. A quick search on the internet revealed that Ken's photos had recorded them being over a thousand kilometres off the migratory path, feeding on flowers they don't usually taste. They were being extremely extraterritorial, putting the world on notice that this place was transforming and that much more was about to come back to life in a new way. The universal billboard had been more significant than we had noticed then.

Butterflies are a universal symbol of regeneration and transformation. They wistfully remind us that sometimes we must perish in one form to return as something much more. We leave behind a heritage for our young. Then we become that young again. This is how reincarnation works. Extinction can be turned around. Dunn's Swamp shows us that. When we protect our young, we are protecting ourselves. Sometimes, things must be hidden to keep the promise of the future safe, but eventually, nothing is lost; it is all in us, and we eternally regenerate just like the butterfly.

THE WHITE GODDESS
The other place I run away to is Fraser Island, soon to be renamed with the indigenous title K'Gari.

Fraser Island/K'Gari is the largest sand island in the world, located off the southeast coast of Queensland. The island has forty lakes with crystal blue water because it is filtered by pure white silica sand. It is a healing place. Lake Mackenzie, one of K'Gari's silica water lakes, had utterly healed my oldest son's severe dermatitis. Things endure a long time here. Two thousand-year-old satinay trees and king ferns that exist nowhere else on the planet stand eternally in the middle of the silently flowing sand streams. The caper white butterflies also populate these creeks. This is the white place for the Butchulla people. White is a colour that represents death and rebirth for most indigenous peoples. Fraser Island is their living Garden of Eden. Their creation legends centre on this island, which they call Princess K'Gari, the White Goddess.

INDIGENOUS CREATION STORY
Their K'Gari dreaming is told this way: -
Beiral, the great sky god, created all the people: animals, humans and plants. Yet, the people had no land. Therefore, Beiral sent Yendingie with a great club to carve out the land from the sea. He sculpted majestic mountains, dug deep fertile valleys, and grew tired. He wandered up the beach to Burleigh Heads, where he slept for a long time. A helper was sent to take care of all the little details. She was a beautiful white spirit of regeneration named Princess K'Gari. She helped make the beautiful places, the seashores, the mountain ranges, the lakes, and the rivers. Princess K'Gari enjoyed what she was doing so much that she fell in love with this world. She told Yendingie, "I think this is the most beautiful place we have ever made. Please, Yendingie, I would like to stay here forever."

Yendingie refused because Princess K'Gari was only a spirit and did not belong to this world. "They will not love you like I do. They will not treat you with the respect that a princess deserves. They will forget what you have done for them and what you have created for them." However, Princess K'Gari pleaded with him, and eventually, Yendingie agreed to let her stay. Yendingie told Princess K'Gari: "I need to change you because you cannot remain in this world in your spirit form." He transformed her into a beautiful island covered in pure white sand, the same colour as her skin. Yendingie made some unique trees and flowers to keep her company. He made many mirrored lakes so she could look into the sky and see what Yendingie was doing. He also made laughing creeks and silent waters, where you can still listen to Princess K'Gari's voice. Finally, Yendingie made the black people for Princess K'Gari to keep her company. He told these people who they were, who K'Gari was, and what they needed to do to respect and look after her. He also taught them the magic of procreation so that their children and their children's children would always be there to keep Princess K'Gari company. It was just as beautiful as the white goddess in spirit form when it was all finished. He could do no better for her. No one could. Then Yendingie returned to the sky with sad tears in his eyes. He was loose in the stream of time and could see all things forward and past that K'Gari did not want to see. He knew what would happen to his love but had to let her choose her sad fate.

For many thousands of years, she was happy. Then the white people came. On the 13th of May 1836, a woman named Eliza Frazer, with the same skin colour as K'Gari, brought chaos to her companions. In 1850, the 3000 indigenous inhabitants began to be removed to the mainland. The logging, mining, and rape of the island started in 1870. Banjo Henry Owens was the last Fraser Island Indigenous to be removed from the mainland; he was sent to the Cherbourg Mission in the 1930s. The island's indigenous population had become extinct. K'Gari was alone, as Yendingie had feared.

In the mid-1960s, rare earths, and precious rich rutile, ilmenite, zircon, and monazite deposits were discovered in K'Gari's sands. Queensland Titanium Mines Pty Ltd and Murphy Ores took out mining leases. Fortunately, the new white people began to defend K'Gari. The battle raged through both the state and federal courts to try to stop her being raped and pillaged. It resulted in "The Fraser Island Environmental Inquiry", which, in October 1976, resulted in the banning of all sand mining, following which she was made a "World Heritage" listed site. The inquiry concluded that:

> "The natural environment of Fraser Island is of great significance, complexity and fragility. The island possesses individual features of great attraction and importance - such as its perched lakes, immense beaches, cliffs of Teewah (coloured) sands, sand blows and rainforested sand dunes. But the inevitable highlighting of the presence and importance of these individual features of its natural environment should not be allowed to obscure the links and interdependency of its many fragile elements, while, overall, an impression of wilderness gives unity to the broad spectrum of the particular natural features of the island."

Today, Princess K'Gari is still there, solitary and alone, off the northeastern coast of Australia, looking up at the sky, missing her dark-skinned companions, and wishing she had listened to Yendingie's wisdom. She dormantly awaits the moment when another transformation will release her from this cocoon of isolation.

THE DARK GODDESS

At Dunn's Swamp is the centre of the universe. It is Nullo Mountain. To the local Wiradjuri people, Nullo Mountain is the big, caring, overseeing matriarch around which the whole universe revolves. I got this concept straight away. I related it to when I visited my girlfriend Julie's childhood home. I remember her father as a jolly, intelligent, but hen-pecked man who could make a joke out of anything. This day, his wife snapped at all of us in the household. He assumed a mock-frightened straight face. "Do as you are asked because in this house, Mother is God!"

In a group of nations where "all mothers are important," Nullo is the mother of all mothers! She sits in the middle of The Wollemi National Park, the largest wilderness in New South Wales, at 487000^2 hectares. It is located 129 kilometres northwest of Sydney and forms a large part of the Greater Blue Mountains World Heritage Area.

Nullo is a dark, squat lump of a mountain that crouches on her haunches and watches over her children: animal, human and plant. She does not lie on her back in the water like K'Gari. The Wiradjuri people were a conquering nation. They are the most significant surviving indigenous language group in Australia. This is because they were the largest mob before the arrival of the white settlers and the convict slaves. As far as the histories can recount, they had more significant numbers of permanent structures and more national trade than any other indigenous language group. They controlled an area larger than the Aztec nation. From the northwest of Sydney, all the way down to Victoria. Their rule was matriarchal. Similar to the Aztecs, strength and fear kept them from being challenged. Evidence of ritualised cannibalism has been found in their past. The other language groups around them speak of this in hushed tones. Nobody wanted to upset The Wiradjuri. Nobody would set foot on their sacred land. Nobody wanted to upset their Great Mother Nullo. No one is sure why the historians do not want you to know that The Wiradjuri were such fierce people with a history of wars, conquest and slavery. Like many other races on the planet, humans can take strong energy and make bad choices. All anybody has to do to find out this history is ask the elders, and they will tell you.

However, this land still commands respect today. UNESCO World Heritage status was granted before this area could be raped. Minerals abound. Ochre-coloured agate lines the shores of her waterways. Deposits of giant calcite crystals are ignored where the coal and lime are mined. Though limited mining takes place nearby, she will never be raped. She is too strong; she will never allow it. She is robust and abundant, actively involved in the preservation of her charges.

Though the history surrounding the dark mother is tainted, she is still a mother. Even a harsh mother is caring and loving. To live and thrive in the Australian bush, one must be tough. Moving through the landscape, you can feel the strength she gives you and the respect she demands in return.

In this place, everything happens when it is needed most. Nullo does nothing by half measures. The methods of her transformations come in full force. She calls to her what is needed. The rains come, and water is

Calcite Crystals at Dunn's Swamp © Ken Wills 25th Nov 2010

stored to bring life back to an unbalanced area. The storing of water helped reverse the process of being extinguished for many of her children: plant, human and animal. The fire sweeps through when it is most needed, bringing to life the things that need fire to procreate.

My biological mother is from this area. Sixty years ago, Nullo transformed me and called me forth from the chrysalis in her womb. Nullo needed something forceful to help bring back respect and interest in the old ways of the people of this land when it was most needed. This would stop them from becoming extinct. Nullo, through my friend Tony Crease, asked me to use my abilities to help rediscover the birthing cave. When I did, Nullo poked me in the eye with a big stick to stop me from entering before I had proper permission. Now that was a surprise! Either Nullo concealed the poke in the eye with a blunt stick from me or spontaneously created it in the stream of time to make sure she got my attention. Either way, she certainly did! I listened and did not enter.

I feel that Nullo called me because I am good at making noise and getting attention. I put on a big event from the 11th to the 14th of November 2011 to ask all Wiradjuri people and people interested in Wiradjuri ways to come back to "On Country," with permission from the elders because the birthing caves had been rediscovered. Because the birthing caves had been rediscovered, it would reverse the process of extinction for the Wiradjuri. It means that the Wiradjuri can transform and would be reborn. They would not disappear like the ones that lived with K'Gari. They would come back to the area and grow strong once again. Nullo called forth butterflies from K'Gari to this area to help me not give up on what I had seen that I must do. Nullo is still calling all of her people back to her. Listen! Can you hear the low, strong, steady call? The same voice called the butterflies to fly a thousand kilometres out of their way. If you are reading this, she is calling you too. Can you hear her?

BIRTH OF THE BUTTERFLIES

Here is a story by Gulpilil, which explains a dreaming time before transformation when no animal, human or plant died and everything stayed the same. All the birds and animals lived forever; no one ever died. None of the creatures knew about death because they had never seen it until a young cockatoo suddenly slipped, fell, and landed on his head. The other animals rushed to help, but the young cockatoo lay very still and didn't move. Was he embarrassed and hiding his face, or perhaps he was having a sleep? They tried to wake him, but he just lay there unmoving.

Eventually, old wombat waddled up and nuzzled the little body lying there. He realised that the young cockatoo had broken his neck. The old wombat called a meeting to which all the animals came. While they were standing around discussing what had happened to the young cockatoo, spirits came, slowly dissolving the little body where it lay, taking it into the sky.

Then the old wombat said, "I think that the spirits have taken the cockatoo up into the sky so they can change him into something else."

Possum said, "Someone should go up into the sky to see what the spirits are doing with the little cockatoo?"

The crows were asked, but they flatly refused. The magpie geese just made excuses and blamed everyone else as their reason for not doing it.

Old wise wombat understood the reason no one was volunteering. It would be lonely and cold that high up in the sky, and there would be no shelter. The old wombat was so busy looking up that he had not looked down, and he had not noticed that the caterpillars had wriggled up and were trying to volunteer.

Image - Caper White On Melaleuca Flower Dunn's Swamp © Ken Wills 27th November 2010

"We could all go together," the caterpillars said with one voice. "If we do, we can make our camp and spend the whole winter there. When it gets warm in the spring, we will return and tell you what is happening to the young cockatoo."

Brilliant! All thanked the caterpillars as they gathered and slowly crawled into the sky in one huge, wriggling cloud.

As spring approached, all the animals began searching for signs of the return of the caterpillars, yet each day passed without any sign at all. Then, on the first warm spring day, a beautiful parade of brightly coloured wings flocked around the camp.

"It is us! It is us! We are the caterpillars transformed. This happens when the spirits take you to the sky after death. Cockatoo has been transformed and will be in his mother's belly again soon too."

The bright colours and fluttering wings made everyone smile at the beauty. Everyone was so happy and not afraid of what might have happened to the young cockatoo any more. The old ones decided that this must always be so. So that people would be reminded not to be afraid and could know what happened after death, the caterpillars would spend winter hidden in cocoons, unmoving like they were dead, preparing for the transformation into their beautiful new form that would make the world a little lighter and brighter.

THE PSYCHE
Psychic is a new word. Before that, we had to use the old words 'witch,' 'occultist,' or 'shaman' to describe people with paranormal abilities. Psychic and its sister words, Psychiatry and Psychology, come from the Greek word psyche. In Greek, it is the word for both the butterfly and the unconscious soul. This implies that the deep unconscious is human nature's most beautiful and fragile part. In legend, the psyche was so refined and wondrous that the god Eros, the god of lust, became besotted with it. The myth of Psyche and Aphrodite describes the Goddess of love's jealous rage against this irresistibly beautiful part of human nature, which the cold Greek gods lacked.

Conversely, Freud described the deep unconscious as "The Id," the most dangerous, repulsive, carnal and impulsive part of the human. For the last 200 years, western psychological theory has laboured under Freud's belief that human nature is little more than a monstrous caterpillar, an enormous grub, and a self-centred, ill-mannered, and ugly child. Yet ancient mythical archetypes show that this is the immature or larval part of human nature and that growth and transformation occur given the correct environment. When in balance with nature, the natural maturation process, after a period of latency, transforms the juvenile grub of the Id into a glorious and mysterious creature.

What are the catalysts to this transformation, and what lessons can we learn from the butterfly?

1. Nurture Yourself – Nurture The Young.

The female butterfly chooses the best and richest environment to lay her eggs. Butterflies journey over vast distances to find the perfect place for their hatchlings. When the young grubs emerge, they find an abundance of everything they need to grow well. Caterpillars can eat several times their body weight each day. At this developmental stage, being self-centred means survival. They have to avoid predators and provide for their own basic needs.

In infancy, the human baby requires more energy and attention than any other juvenile creature. The gorgeous little human grubs will scream demands and be very self-centred to get their primary survival needs to be met. Unlike Freud's Id, the human child, like the caterpillar, is defenceless and harmless. Grubby Id-like characteristics only continue whilst vulnerability and neediness continue. A good human mother, like a butterfly, ensures her child has the best possible environment for growth. She will also spend the time and energy to ensure that the child receives the lessons on how to successfully protect and nurture itself so that when the infant reaches maturity, it will no longer be dependent upon anyone else for its basic needs.

2. Create Your Own Safe Haven

Like the caterpillar forming its chrysalis, we must create our own solitude fortress. Transformation occurs when we are alone in nature and can reflect upon our life experiences thus far. It is not a bad thing to withdraw into nature and regroup. This allows positive personal growth and change. Find a regenerative sacred place for your revival, like tours or retreats.

3. Strive To Be Your Own Ideal

The stress and struggle that the butterfly experiences as it emerges from its pupa raises its blood pressure and forces fluid into the wings, allowing them to unfold. Struggling for growth causes us to grow and reach a new potential that we did not realise was within us. Like the butterfly's new wings, this is very attractive.

4. Stretch Your Wings Cautiously

When a butterfly unfurls its wings for the first time, it carefully fans the air. It begins trying out this new gift cautiously with slow, tentative movements, gently increasing the speed. First, it will get enough lift to raise one leg. Then it rests. Then it flaps a little harder and raises two legs, holding on firmly with the other feet until it feels safe. When its wings flapping reaches approximately 80km per hour, and controlled flight is possible, it will still hang on with one foot until it feels in control of this new ability. Eventually, it becomes airborne. It is free and confident, and a new life begins.

Just like butterflies, we should not step off into empty air. Plummeting to the ground is not the freedom of flight. We do not want to break our silly cockatoo neck. We should proceed with caution, learning our new abilities and getting used to our wings by lifting one foot in front of the other.

5. Taste Life With Your Feet
No, that doesn't mean: 'Always wear great shoes.' However, that can't be a bad thing! However, butterflies taste with their feet. This makes it easy to see if where they land will be nourishing and yummy. Humans will often stay stuck in stagnant situations. A change can be refreshing and wholesome for our souls.

6. Care For Yourself
Butterflies age via damage to their wings. Once it can no longer spread its wings, its life is as good as over. Therefore, butterflies strive to find shelter from damaging forces. As humans, if we don't place ourselves in harm's way, we can live long, free and colourful lives.

THE BUTTERFLY'S ULTIMATE LESSON
A butterfly's life is short but joyous. It travels the world, floating effortlessly on the warm air currents. It feasts on the sweetest nectar. It will couple with its mate as often as possible and give birth in ecstasy. It wears the promise of the rainbow on its back. Its inner beauty matches its outer beauty, and to have one pass your way, however briefly, is a blessing. As we humans pass through life, if we can leave one person uplifted in our wake by inner beauty, our psyche, or if our gifts can improve a moment in another's existence, then we have learned how to give the magic of the butterfly to another in the same way that Nullo called the butterflies to me.

©Copyright Rev. Dr S. D'Montford Friday, May 30th 2008 Sydney Australia. Modified Wednesday, May 4, 2011

Shé and the endangered Bird Wing Butterfly - © Ken Wills 11th Jan 2007

AUSTRALIAN BUSH TUCKER

Not all native foods will be to your liking, but experiment with these basic bush food recipes to discover which appeal to your taste buds!

WARNING!
Native flora and fauna are protected.
When gathering food for a campsite outside of the National Park, it's essential to be aware of the laws in your state regarding protected species. Most native animals, and even some feral introduced species, require a valid hunting or fishing permit that complies with the state's regulations. However, if you are accompanied by someone who identifies as indigenous, you may not need a permit. It's always better to be safe than sorry, so research before setting out on your trip.

NATIVE FRUITS & VEGGIES

WARRIGAL SPINACH
This is my favourite green vegetable, Warrigal spinach. When eaten raw, it has a zesty taste and a milder flavour when cooked. It can be found growing like a weed along most beaches. The indigenous people used it medicinally to improve eyesight, and Captain Cook used it as a tonic for scurvy. It is also a pretty ground cover to add to your veggie garden. Cook's botanist, Sir Joseph Banks, took spinach seeds back to England, where it is now grown as a summer green. Warrigal (Dharug language, meaning "wild") spinach is known as the first Australian food plant to be cultivated in Europe. There are many names for this nutritious plant, including Warrigal spinach, New Zealand spinach, Botany Bay spinach, Warrigal greens, or wild spinach. This arrowhead-shaped, green-leafed spinach is common in coastal vegetation and is often seen near sandy areas and mangrove swamps. Like most leafy green vegetables, it can be seared and served with a main course of emu or kangaroo or used in salads, roulades, pastry bases, and soups.

Spinach Soup
- A handful of spinach leaves per person
- The same proportion of peeled potatoes
- Dried onion flakes
- Native peppercorns
- Salt
- Sufficient water to cover the ingredients

Method: Start by heating a saucepan of water over hot coals and blanch the spinach for about three minutes. Discard the water and chop the spinach. Then, add about a litre of water to the clean saucepan and bring it to a boil. Put the potatoes in and cook them until they fall apart. Next, add the chopped spinach, peppercorns, and salt to the saucepan. Gently mash the potatoes and let the mixture simmer for another 20 minutes, always ensuring enough liquid.

Warrigal Greens - Tetragonia tetragonioides

Image Royalty Free

MACADAMIA NUTS

Macadamia nuts are the first commercially grown native food in Australia. They were named after John MacAdam, a scientist who studied their nutritional content. Both indigenous people and early settlers considered them an excellent food source. The nuts contain about 70% fat, but most are monounsaturated fat. They are also high in protein. In Queensland, macadamia trees can grow up to 20 meters tall. Although they are large trees, they can be grown in domestic gardens for the nuts and to block out neighbouring views. Macadamia trees can take up to five years to produce fruit, but they can be quite prolific once they start. Nuts appear between six to nine months after flowering. The nut's case is hard to break, even when the husk is removed. If you have a small G-clamp in your camping gear, it is the most effective way to crack macadamia nuts. Like many native foods, the less done to them, the better. Macadamia nuts are delicious when eaten raw or roasted over a campfire. However, they are such versatile ingredients that they can be used in butter, oils, jams, vegetables, fruit salads, breads, and ice creams.

WATTLE

The wattle is the background element in Australia's Coat of Arms. It is a type of acacia that produces clusters of yellow flowers, with hundreds of different species available. Wattle seeds are now commercially available, have a nutty, coffee-like flavour, and are protein-rich. They are used in bread, cones, creams, pavlovas, ice creams, jellies, pancakes, blinis, sauces, chutneys, cakes, mousse, and tea. If you are in the bush and have collected and roasted wattle seeds, brew some wattle tea, giving you a nicer buzz than caffeine.

Wattle Billie Tea
- 4 heaped teaspoons of wattle seeds
- 1 roasting pan
- 1 medium billy ⅔ full of water

Method: Here is a fun way to make bush-made tea. Start by placing a billy, a pot used exclusively to boil water on the campfire, on hot coals to heat it. Then, put a roasting pan alongside the billy and dry roast the wattle seeds for a few minutes. Be sure to oversee the seeds so that they don't burn. Once the seeds are roasted, tip them into the hot water and stir with a green gumtree stick. The stick's gum flavour will slightly add to the tea's flavour. Bring the tea to the boil, strain it, and enjoy a healthy and rewarding cuppa with your camping crew.

BUNYA NUT
Scientific studies have shown that the bunya nut found in Queensland has zero fat content. Moreover, it has slow-releasing carbohydrate properties, making it an ideal food for people with diabetes. These nuts come from the bunya pine tree found in the rainforest. The tree resembles the Hoop and Norfolk Island pine but has spikes. During autumn, the tree sheds cones that are full of seeds. Once husked, these seeds look like the most giant pine nuts you have ever seen. The nuts have a taste similar to that of young waxy potatoes and are pretty filling. They were a significant food source for the local Indigenous population. When you are exploring the southern Queensland highlands or nearby parks, keep an eye out for fallen bunya pine cones. However, avoid parking your car or camping under them during autumn, as the pinecones can weigh between 3-10 kg and cause significant damage to anything underneath them. The bunya nuts can be used in various ways, such as soups, pies, desserts, and sweets.

Bunya Mash
This is my absolute favourite bush tucker. In February, the large Bunya cones will drop. Listen for the crash! You don't have to be in the Queensland Alps to find them, as birds have distributed these seeds into many rainforests. One Bunya pine cone can contain hundreds of large Bunya nuts. Boil them in your camp oven, and then crack open the nuts to relish the nutty, buttery deliciousness. When hot and soft, mash them for a sweet, nutty-flavoured alternative to mashed potato. Yum!

Bunya Pine Nuts - Araucaria Bidwillii - Edible

Image Royalty Free

Bunya Toffee

If you are in a remote location craving a sweet, toffee-like treat, try making this simple recipe.
- 2 pannikins (large metal camping cups) bunya bunya nuts
- 1½ pannikins sugar
- ¼ pannikin Aussie golden syrup
- ½ pannikin water

Method: To make this sweet nut energy and precious bar for bush walks, start by boiling the bunya nuts. Once boiled, let them cool, peel their shells and cut the nuts in half. Grease a hot plate, then place the halved nuts on it. In a saucepan over coals, combine sugar, syrup, and water. Stir the mixture without boiling for about 10 minutes or until the sugar dissolves and thickens. Remove the saucepan from the heat and pour the mixture over the nuts. Let the mixture cool and set. Once set, break up the toffee and enjoy your homemade sweet nut-chew energy bar.

BUSH TOMATO

Bush tomatoes are several nightshade plants (Solanum) native to Australia and belong to the same genus as tomatoes, eggplant, and potatoes. Most of them are edible, but some can be toxic. Therefore, if you are unsure, it's better not to eat them. The good ones have a sweet tamarillo-like flavour, which is why they are also called desert raisins or kutjera. Due to the hot central Australian sun, they sometimes dehydrate on the shrub and resemble raisins while still being edible and retaining their tangy sweetness. It's great to see bush foods regenerate quickly as the demand for bush tucker increases. Young bush tomatoes can be found sprouting along the side of new roadworks. They make a good sauce and can be used as a delicious substitute or in addition to a tin of tomatoes or tomato soup in bush cooking.

Always be careful when eating wild tomato plants. Identifying them adequately is essential; nowadays, it's easier with the Internet. You can take a photo and compare it with species online. Some of the different species can be tricky.

Australian Bush Tomato - Solanum Lithophilum - Edible

Image by Mark Marathon from WikiCommons

Several solanum species contain significant levels of solanine, which can be toxic. It's strongly recommended that people unfamiliar with the plant refrain from experimenting with the different species, as differentiating between them can often be tricky. Some of the edible species are:

- Solanum aviculare kangaroo apple
- Solanum centrale, desert raisin, bush raisin, bush sultana, the native name kutjera
- Solanum chippendalei bush tomato, named after botanist George Chippendale
- Solanum diversiflorum bush tomato, karlumbu, pilirta, wamurla
- Solanum ellipticum potato bush
- Solanum laciniatum kangaroo apple.
- Solanum orbiculatum round-leaved solanum
- Solanum phlomoides wild tomato.

In 1859, Indigenous people were observed burning off the outer skin of S. aviculare as the raw state would blister their mouths. S. chippendalei is consumed by splitting the fruit, scraping the centre out and eating the outer flesh, as the seeds and surrounding placenta are bitter. S.

diversiflorum is roasted before being eaten or dried. The fruit of S.orbiculatum is edible, but the fruit of the large-leafed form may be bitter. The fruit of S. phlomoides appears edible after removing seeds and roasting or sun drying.

Desert Tomato Soup
- 1 large tin of tomatoes or tomato soup
- ½ 2-1 pannikin (lg tin cup) bush tomatoes
- Native peppercorns and salt
- Local herbs
- 1 pannikin water

Method: Using a fork to make a delicious soup over hot coals, start by mashing tinned tomatoes in a camp oven. If you use tomato soup, you must add more water. Add finely chopped bush tomatoes, seasonings, herbs, a crumbled stock cube, and water. Simmer the mixture for at least half an hour until the soup thickens. The cooking time may vary depending on the heat of the coals. This soup makes a great drink or meal around the campfire.

BOAB TREE

The baobab tree, also known as the bottle tree, has a thick, round trunk with hollows that can hold water. These trees act as fluid reservoirs and have been lifesavers in the desert. The bottle-shaped tree is stout and not very tall, with branches similar in shape but not as thick. The round, gourd-like fruit has edible and meaty pulp with many seeds buried inside. These seeds can be eaten fresh or roasted separately and served like peanuts. They can also be used for sprouting. After consuming a plentiful meal from the baobab's abundant crop, the indigenous people mix the tree's sap with water to make a drink.

Australian Bob Tree - Adansonia Gregorii

Image Royalty Free

Roasted Boab Fruit and Seeds
- An immature Boab fruit (greenish rather than brown, on gourd-like skin)

Method: Place the fruit on the warm coals. If the coals are too hot, the fruit may explode. Gently roast until the warm pulp is like stewed fruit when broken open.

Did you know Boab seeds can be roasted in a wooden coolamon or dish? A coolamon is usually made from wood or bark and is commonly used by indigenous peoples to carry things. To roast the seeds, place warm coals and Boab seeds in the coolamon and toss them until they're cooked. This is a great way to enjoy this tasty snack!

LILLYPILLY

The lilly pilly (Eugenia smithii) is an Australian native tree often grown as a street tree or planted in gardens across Victoria to Queensland. These trees produce edible white, lilac or purple berries, which can be difficult to pick due to the height of the trees. However, lillypilly fruit is abundant, and many fall to the ground. As long as they are not bruised, they can be used to make jellies, glazes, tarts, and vinegar or served as a side dish with fish and meat.

Lillypillies have a watermelon-like texture, but their taste ranges from sour to strong, cinnamon and clove-like. When preserved, their flavour becomes less intense. Interestingly, the Victorian lillypilly is excellent for making vinegar, whereas, on the far north coast of New South Wales, lillypillies are too strong to be used by themselves. Instead, their fruit is made into jams, chutneys, and jellies or used as a sauce on red or white meat.

If you are out in the bush and come across many lillypillies with a few hours to spare, a lillypilly vinegar can easily accompany your catch of the day.

Lillypilly Vinegar
- 2kg lillypillies, plain or mixed
- 3 litres white wine vinegar
- 1 camp oven

Method: Please note the following instructions. You can adjust the quantities depending on how much lillypilly you have. Cooking is all about ratios, so try to maintain the same ratio. Place the camp oven on hot coals, add vinegar and fruit, and let it simmer for about two hours. After that, let it cool down a bit, and then strain it using a muslin cloth or any other available material. If you have any leftover vinegar with oriental spice flavour, put it in an empty bottle for future use.

RIBERRY

Riberries, or small-leafed clove lillypilly fruit, are commonly used in fruit tarts. Some riberries have seeds, while others are seedless, and the seedless ones are preferred. If you find riberries while on a bushwalk, you can pick them and make a sauce for your dinner.

Riberry Sauce
- Riberries
- Meat or vegetable stock
- Water

Method: After cooking your camp oven meal, remove it from the oven, but keep the stock aside. Add a small amount of water, crush the riberry fruit and add it to the oven. Allow the liquid to reduce and the fruit to soften. At this point, the liquid should have a shiny, glaze-like consistency. Serve this nutritious sauce as a complement to your main meal.

MUNTRI (KUNZEA)

The indigenous people living by the sea had access to seafood and bush fruits. They often combine the two to create unique and delicious dishes. One such fruit is the small, lemon apple-flavoured, furry berry known as the muntri or native cranberry. This fruit, along with cloves and guavas, belongs to the Myrtle family and has a subtle cinnamon crab apple flavour. It can be eaten fresh, in fruit pies, or sauces. When ripe, the small green berry turns brown to pink and tastes like an apple. Muntries are great pickled or used in many sweet or savoury applications, such as sauces and chutneys. They can also be brewed into a lovely tea. The plant is a ground-cover creeper with white, spiky spring and early summer blossoms. When the muntries produce their pea-sized fruit, you will be drawn to the pleasant, apple-smelling dunes.

Native Muntri Sauce
- Muntries
- ¼ pannikin oil
- 3 drops edible eucalyptus oil
- 2 lemon myrtle or lemon-flavoured herbs
- Salt
- 2 tbsp butter, optional

Method: If you're cooking meat or fish and want to make a sauce, you can use the remaining liquid in the pan to create a flavourful sauce. Just place the pan on a campfire, mix two oils, and add butter and the oil mixture to the pan. Next, add muntries, lemon myrtle leaves, or herbs and toss until the mixture is reduced and cooked. This will result in a creative and delicious bush-flavoured sauce.

PIGFACE
Pigface grows on the dunes and coastal cliffs of eastern Australia. Produces bright purple, daisy-like flowers and reddish-purple fruit. All plant parts, including the flowers, fruit, and leaves, are edible. However, the fruit is the most delicious and is often enjoyed by Indigenous Australians. Why this awesomely tangy, sweet/salty native fruit hasn't taken the world by storm is beyond me. Or maybe it's a good thing for us foraging types. The leaves of this edible native succulent can be eaten raw or stir-fried. The fruit is purple when ripe in late summer and has a salty and sweet taste, making it a delicious snack. The fruit contains a lot of drinkable moisture, and its juice, similar to aloe vera, can be used to soothe burns, bites, and stings. The fleshy, juicy leaves taste slightly salty and can be used as a salt substitute in salads or as an accompaniment to meat, seafood, or egg dishes. After the flowers fall off, there is a red calyx left. Peel the calyx like a banana. The tough outer skin of the fruit is discarded, and the tangy fruit inside can be eaten raw or cooked. The sticky sap inside the leaves can be rubbed on insect bites, jellyfish stings, and sunburn to soothe the skin. The flesh of the fruit has a slightly gelatinous texture similar to kiwi fruit, strawberry, or even a fig with a salty twist. It can also be used in pickles, chutneys, or jams.

Pickled Pigface
- 1 cup hot water
- 100 ml vinegar
- ⅓ cup sugar
- 1 tsp salt

- Orange or lemon peel
- 2 bay leaf
- 1 tsp black peppercorn
- 2 handfuls pigface, thinly sliced

Method: Mix hot water and vinegar with sugar and salt in a bowl to prepare a pickling solution. Stir the mixture until the sugar and salt have completely dissolved. Next, add your citrus peel, bay leaf, peppercorns and pigface in a large jar. Pour the hot liquid mixture over the pigface and spices. Let it sit for at least 15 minutes or until it cools down. Once done, store it in the fridge.

Pigface - Carpobrotus Glaucescens - Edible

Image Royalty Free

ROSELLA FLOWER

The Australian rosella parrot is not considered to be a good food option. A common joke is that if you catch one, you should put it in a pot with a rock and boil it all day. After finishing, throw away the bird and eat the rock instead! However, the native rosella fruit is quite delicious. It is a small shrub called Hibiscus heterophyllus found in the damp forest areas of eastern Australia. The native rosella is a beneficial vegetable as well. The leaves of the plant taste like sorrel and can be used in pastry or as an herb, while the roots have a flavour similar to that of a parsnip. The yellow or white flowers of the shrub can be eaten raw, mixed in salads, or used in chutney. The whole red flower also looks and tastes excellent when floating in the bottom of a glass of champagne. Additionally, the rosella buds make excellent jam with a flavour comparable to a plum. Some studies have shown that it can help control blood pressure. However, it should be kept in mind that pregnant women should avoid consuming it as it contains a hormone that can trigger a miscarriage.

Rosella Jam
- Ripe rosella fruit
- Raw sugar

- Filtered water
- Lemon juice, just a squeeze

Method: Firstly, remove the red leaves (es) from the seed pods, then wash and drain them separately. Slightly break open the pods and put them in a small saucepan. Pour enough water to cover them and ensure they're completely submerged. Cover the saucepan and bring the water to a boil. Cook the pods for about 20 minutes or until they become soft. Strain the liquid and discard the seed pods. Pour the reserved liquid back into the saucepan and add the washed calyxes. If the calyxes are not covered in water, add more water. Boil the mixture again for another 20 minutes until it thickens. Estimate the volume of cooked pulp and add the same amount of sugar and a squeeze of lemon juice. Boil the mixture for 10-20 minutes or until the jam thickens. Transfer the jam to a clean jar and let it cool. Store it in the refrigerator. If you overcook the jam and it becomes too firm in the jar, it's perfect for slicing and serving with cheese, much like quince paste.

QUANDONG

The Quandong (Santalum acuminatum), also known as native peach, is primarily found in the arid regions of southern Australia. The fruit has a sweet and slightly acidic flavour and is a good source of vitamin C. The early settlers

of Australia used the seeds present in the fruit to make beads, buttons, and game tokens. The kernel of the fruit can be eaten either fresh or roasted. The tree can grow well in semi-arid and well-watered areas, making it particularly beneficial. The red fruit of the Quandong is used for making jams and jellies and can be stewed as a fruit.

Stewed Quandongs
- Quandongs
- Sugar to sweeten slightly
- Water

A rough idea for the fruit/sugar ratio is 1 pannikin of sugar per 400g of freshly pitted fruit.

Method: To prepare quandongs, place a heavy-duty saucepan over hot coals and add the fruits, sugar, and enough water to cover them. Gently simmer the fruits until they become soft and have a plum/peach-like texture while having a slightly acidic taste. You can enjoy the quandongs with their delicately flavoured juices. To add extra flavour and texture, mix in some chopped macadamia nuts.

NATIVE PLUMS

Australian bush plums, such as The Davidson, Illawarra, and Kakadu varieties, can make jams, tarts, sauces, and glazes. These trees grow in the rainforests of New South Wales and Queensland. The Illawarra purple/brown plum, also known as the brown pine plum, has a seed on the outside, and the edible area is the larger, swollen stem. The Kakadu plum, found in the Kakadu region of the Northern Territory, is the most nutritious of the native plums. It has the highest fruit source of vitamin C in the world. The fruit can be harvested in tropical and desert regions and used in soups, such as kangaroo tail, or stewed.

NATIVE HERBS AND SPICES
Other ingredients used in these recipes include:

Native Peppers
Also known as Tasmannia lanceolata, it grows small branches of pinky-red fruits. The seeds from these fruits can be ground into pepper and used in sweet and savoury dishes. Mountain pepper berry trees can grow up to 4-5 meters and prefer cooler climates. Both the leaves and the berries of this tree are edible. When the berries are eaten fresh, they taste sweet, followed by a hot, peppery taste. However, beware that this hot taste is strong, so be careful. The leaves stems, and berries have an aromatic, peppery flavour and contain approximately three times the antioxidants of blueberries.

Lemon Aspen
Also known as Acronychia acidula, it is a small to medium-sized rainforest tree that is endemic to Queensland. It has simple, elliptical leaves, small groups of flowers in leaf axils, and more or less spherical fruit. The fruit is aromatic and acidic and is harvested as a bush food. It is commonly found in the rainforests of the eastern coast of Australia. The small yellow fruit has a citrus tang and is often used as a substitute for lemon juice. In contrast, the native lime grows in drier areas.

Lemon Myrtle
Also known as Backhousia citriodora, it is a beautiful Australian shrub that naturally occurs in the wetter coastal areas of northern New South Wales and southern Queensland. The lemon-scented leaves contain citral, making them rich in antioxidants and Vitamin C, giving your food a unique citrus flavour. It has a large seed and a thin but delicious flesh that can be eaten raw.

Paperbark
It is the name given to several small trees in the myrtle family belonging to the genus Melaleuca, characterised by their whitish papery bark. Using it as a natural wrap for your food while cooking can add a unique earthy flavour to your dishes. Additionally, paperbark has sanitising properties.

Green Gum-Tree Sticks
can be used to stir your food while cooking, giving your dish a subtle and refreshing eucalyptus flavour.

FISH & SEAFOOD

NATIVE SEAFOOD DELICACIES
The large heaps of debris left by corroborees, known as midden heaps, are composed of seafood shells that have accumulated over centuries. These historical midden heaps can be found along the Australian coastline, indicating that our indigenous ancestors deeply loved Australian seafood, much like we do today.

Australian Rock Oysters
are widely known for their delicious taste around the world. They are smaller than other varieties and can survive without water for a few weeks while still in their shell. You can harvest oysters from Tin Can Bay in Queensland down to Victoria's Mallacoota Inlet. However, the laws for wild oysters permit you to eat as many oysters as you wish on the spot, but they don't allow you to take them home or back to your campfire. The best way to enjoy oysters is to serve them raw and clean, with only lemon juice, salt, and ground pepper. This simple yet fantastic meal is perfect for campers.

Bugs
Morton Bay or Balmain Bugs are a flat marine lobster with tender, sweet flesh that makes for a fantastic meal when boiled in clean, fresh water.

PIPIS
You can find wedge-shaped molluscs, called Pipis, living just a few centimetres below the beach's surface. It's a fun activity for kids to wiggle and twist their feet in the wet sand to collect them for dinner, giving them the feeling of contributing to the camping trip. Before cooking, clean and soak them in cold water to remove sand. Pipis can be boiled or barbecued.

Pipi Chowder
Pipis are shellfish that live in the sand between the high and low tide levels on the beach. They belong to the cockle family. People who enjoy eating pipis usually clean them and then marinate them in lemon or native lime juice before wrapping them up in damper.
- About 20 pipis
- 300 ml milk
- seasoned flour
- native herbs

Method: To prepare the pipis, soak them in fresh water for approximately two hours to remove sand. Then, add the pipis to a camp oven on hot coals with about 1cm of water. When the shells open, add 600ml of water and simmer for approximately 10 minutes. After that, strain the mixture and add milk. Add cream or blend milk with seasoned flour to thicken the mix. Finally, serve the dish and sprinkle it with native herbs for added flavour.

CRABS

Australian crabs are plentiful and an excellent food source. If you're camping near the beach, remember to take a crab pot and place it near the mangroves for the chance of catching a tasty mud crab. The stunningly-coloured blue swimmers can be caught with a standard fishing line near the mangrove estuary. Boil them soon after catching them for maximum flavour.

Blue Swimmers and Beer

- 1 or 2 blue swimmer crabs per person
- Salt

Method: Blue swimmer crabs must be soaked in water for an hour before cooking. To prepare, boil plenty of water in a camp oven, add salt and the crabs, and boil for 15 minutes. Once done, let the crabs cool.

You can serve crabs with salad greens or vegetables. Cut the crab's body around the edges and pop the top off. Remove the meat using a sharp, pointed knife. Use a hammer to gently crack the claws and legs so that you can get all the meat out and serve the meat with a can of cold beer!

MUSSELS

The Victorian coastline and Tasmania are home to mussels and bi-valve shellfish found in inlets and bays south of about 30 degrees latitude. Ensuring the mussels are fresh before preparing them for a meal is essential. The shells should be closed; if they are only slightly open, you can tap them with your finger. If they close straight away, they are safe to use. Discard any that remain open, as the animal inside may be dead and not fresh.

Always consume seafood while it is fresh because food poisoning on a camping trip can be unpleasant. It is essential to wash the mussel carefully and remove its fibrous, clinging beard. Once cooked, the mussels will re-open. You can barbecue or steam them in a camp oven with water or a little white wine and herbs. Be careful not to put too many mussels in the oven; allow room for them to open. Cover the camp oven with a lid and simmer for a few minutes. Even in the bush, you can serve mussels in many ways. They make a particularly easy hors d'oeuvre when wrapped in bacon and quickly heated over hot coals.

Mussels, Rice and (Bush) Tomatoes
- 20 mussels or as many as you like, beards removed
- 10 ripe bush tomatoes or prepared tomato chutney
- 3 cups cooked rice
- Local herbs

Method: Place a heavy-duty saucepan over hot coals and heat two cups of salted water. Boil rice in the saucepan. While the rice is cooking, prepare the tomatoes and mussels. Although bush tomatoes are more commonly found in the north, you can still make a delicious topping by heating a chutney with a few herbs. If you have bush tomatoes, chop them up and simmer them in water or wine with herbs until they reduce and thicken.

Next, place a camp oven over the hot coals. Add water, wine, and herbs to the oven and steam the mussels for a few minutes. Once the mussels are cooked, drain them and place them on the rice in their shells. Finally, pour the thickened tomatoes over the mussels and rice for a delicious meal. Enjoy!

PRAWNS
Prawns are primarily found in the warmer northern waters of Australia. The eastern king prawn, which is quite popular, can be found along the east coast of Australia from Lakes Entrance in Victoria to the North Reef in Queensland. They are usually caught during the spring and summer in estuaries. One should wade in shallow waters with a hand-held net and a bright light to attract prawns. Prawns have delicate flavours; therefore, the most straightforward cooking preparation usually provides the best results. Heavy ingredients served with prawns tend to be too dominant and may overpower their delicate flavours.

Grilled Prawns with Native Citrus
- Green prawns, as many as you can eat
- Lemon aspen fruit, lemon myrtle or lemon-scented tea tree leaves, native limes or lemons

Method: It is possible to cook whole prawns simply by placing them on a greased cast iron plate on hot coals. You can baste them with citrus juice or add citrus leaves to the cooking plate to infuse more flavour into the prawns. If you prefer to shell the prawns before cooking, remove the dark tract that runs down the back of the tail. Shelling the prawns has an additional benefit, as you can use the shells to make soup stock.

WASTE NOT WANT NOT
- r e m e m b e r -
All your leftovers can become great burly and bait for catching more food to feed everyone around your campfire.
Dispose of any unwanted scraps responsibly.
Don't leave scraps around any campsite, as they can attract unwelcome guests like rats, seagulls, feral pigs and feral ibis.

BARRAMUNDI
Australia is often called 'Down Under', but we Aussies are proud of our Top End, where the barramundi fish thrives in warm waters. It can be caught along the northern coast of Western Australia and the northern waters of Queensland. The name 'barramundi' comes from the Tjabaki language, which means 'large-scaled river fish'. It's also known as barramunda or giant perch and is a type of Australian lungfish with paddle-like fins and a long body. The fish can be found in fresh and salt waters and has a blue-grey upper body, while its silver sides have a yellowish tinge. Barramundi has firm, sweet white flesh and can be cooked with wild ginger, in paperbark, or baked on hot coals.

Barramundi in Paperbark
This recipe mainly requires gum leaves and paperbark, which are easily accessible. Gum trees are abundant in Australia, and the commonly known Melaleuca tree has papery bark. Native limes are usually found in dry rainforests or arid areas. They are indigenous citrus. There are several varieties. They are superb.
- 1 barramundi
- 2 native limes (optional)
- Gum leaves
- Paperbark

Method: To cook barramundi, scale, gut it, and then rinse it thoroughly. Rub lime all over the fish. Take some paperbark and dampen it. Place a thin layer of gum leaves between the fish and the bark, and fully wrap the barramundi in the bark, ensuring it is covered. Move some fire coals away and dig a hole about 30 cm deep underneath the fire. Place a layer of coals at the bottom of the hole, and then put the fish on top of the coals. Cover the fish with the remaining coals. Seal the coals with either sand or dirt and leave for about one to one and a half hours, depending on the size of the fish.

Whole Barramundi in Coals
- 1 whole barramundi, gutted
- Bed of hot coals
- Paperbark or banana leaf plates
- Gum leaves for resting fish

Method: Leave the scales on the whole barramundi to protect its delicious meat and make timing easier. Place the gutted barramundi on scorching coals and turn it frequently to avoid burning. The cooking time will depend on the fish's size and the coals' heat. Once the flesh turns white, remove the fish from the fire and place it on gum leaves or any available fresh leaves. Insert a knife along the backbone, halve the fish, and remove the bones. Remember to eat the cheek, as it is considered a prime cut.

SALMON

Although Atlantic salmon is not native to Australia, it was introduced into the lakes, rivers, and dams of New South Wales with limited success. In the 1900s, Atlantic salmon farming began in southern Tasmania; today, it has become a thriving business. Tasmanian Atlantic salmon is now considered one of the Australian food delicacies. The salmon farms are worth visiting if you are in south Tasmania. The salmon's flesh is pinkish-apricot and has a delicate and distinctive flavour.

Salmon Over Coals
- 1 salmon, gutted and cut into cutlets
- Butter

Method: Although salmon is oily, it can dry quickly when cooked on a grill or in a pan. Rub salmon cutlets with butter and place them on a char grill over hot coals to prevent this. Cook for approximately four minutes on each side, adjusting the cooking time according to the cutlet's thickness and the coals' heat. It is best to eat the salmon immediately after cooking.

Poached Camp Salmon
- 1x 3 kg whole salmon
- A camp oven or poacher, with a rack
- Native peppercorn leaves

Method: You'll need enough hot coals and ashes to cook your fish over an open fire. Fill a container with around 3cm of water and bring it to a boil. Once boiling, place a rack over the water and position your fish on it. Monitor the water level to ensure it doesn't boil dry. Allow the fish to poach for about an hour. Finally, garnish your salmon with native peppercorn leaves to add some pizazz.

TROUT

Trout, an introduced species, is now commonly found across Australia. Commercial hatcheries breed trout, and state governments release them into public waters. The famous rainbow and brown trout are prolific in Australia's cooler southern waters. Brown trout becomes a more dominant species when sharing water with rainbow trout. Ocean trout farming is now thriving in Tasmania.

Coral trout are found in coral reef waters around Queensland, the Northern Territory and Western Australia. They are easily recognised by the small blue spots on their body and head, ranging from pink to reddish-brown. Coral trout can grow up to 20 kg, and their white flesh is delicious when cooked. If you are camping by a mountain stream and wake up early, pan-fried trout makes a beautiful breakfast. However, it is essential to cook the trout sparingly as it can lose its delicate flavour and become too dry to enjoy.

Trout in the Mud
- 1 large trout
- Mud or clay to cover fish

Method: Place some newspaper on the ground to cook a moist and delicious trout. You can use any paper without coating. To test this, place a corner of the paper in the fire and watch if any coating melts or peels off it. Make sure you lay the paper. Then, shape a mud or clay mould around the fish, ensuring the mud is about 1.5 cm thick. If you wrap meat in mud or clay without paper, ensure the mud coating is thicker.

Next, dig a hollow in the coals and place the mud-coated fish inside. Cover it with coals and ashes and cook for approximately 45 minutes. Once done, remove the mud-fish and let the casing cool until you can smash it. This will cause the skin and scales to come away from the fish, leaving you with a beautifully moist trout.

Finally, remove the small lump inside the fish, the gut. Serve the trout while still relatively hot, and enjoy!

MULLET
The sea mullet is one of Australia's most commonly found edible food. It has an olive-green top and silvery sides that help it to blend in with its surroundings. It can be easily found in all states of Australia except Tasmania. An average-sized fish weighs around 1 kg and is about 45 cm long. The flesh of sea mullet is delicious and can be cooked in various ways, such as smoking, frying, or grilling. The flat-tail mullet, also known as jumping mullet, is a common fish found in fresh to brackish water in estuaries around Australia, except Tasmania. It is light brown with a

silvery underbelly and is around 30 cm long. The oily flesh of the flat-tail mullet has a distinct flavour that fish lovers either like or dislike. There are minimal restrictions on catching mullet; they vary slightly state by state, so check before you fish. It is easy to catch. While serious fishermen may not prize it, it is a beneficial bush food. One can easily catch it by jagging it on a line using bread wrapped in a circle of elastic with hooks on the outer edges, making it easy to get bait or a quick feed.

Mullet in Banana Leaves Over Coals

As bananas are widespread from northern New South Wales to Queensland, travellers have a good chance of finding banana leaves in the area. Another good option is paperbark.
- 2 average-sized mullet
- 1 native lime or lemon
- Native peppercorns and salt, to taste
- Banana leaves

Method: To prepare the mullet, you must first scale and clean it. Then, make shallow slashes across the fish and insert slivers of lime or lemon. Place the remaining citrus in the fish cavity, rub the fish with salt, and place peppercorns or leaves around it. Next, lay the mullet on individual banana leaves, sprinkle water, and wrap it. Tie it firmly with banana leaf strips. Put it in warm coals and cook it for 30-40 minutes. Towards the end of cooking, open the leaves. When ready to serve, the skin will lift easily, and the flesh will flake. Place charred leaves and cooked fish on a fresh banana leaf plate if you have any leftover banana leaves.

TILAPIA

Tilapia is an introduced fish species in Australia. It was intentionally brought here by Asian communities as a food source and introduced into local waterways, causing devastation among our native fish breeds. Although it is a good-eating fish, it is a feral species that needs to be removed. If you catch one, even if you're not hungry, please do not throw it back in. You are doing Australia a favour by removing this invasive species. There are no bag limits or size limits on Tilapia, so you can catch and eat as much as you like. You can get a chart identifying introduced species at most bait and tackle shops.

CROCODILE

Okay, technically, it is a lizard. But if you have ever witnessed a three-meter saltwater crocodile chasing after your boat as you pull out into Darwin Harbour, you'll probably consider it a seafood because you should eat it before it eats you. The Indigenous knew that large crocodiles were not problematic to catch at any time, but after significant floods, crocodiles were often stranded in small waterholes and could be speared easily. The indigenous only sometimes hunted saltwater crocodiles for food. Those who did value the tail for its fat and flavour and ground the backbone for vital minerals like phosphorous and calcium, which balanced their dairy-free diet. Nowadays, both freshwater and saltwater crocodiles are farmed in pens until they reach about two metres in length. They are then slaughtered, and every part of the animal is honoured and utilised. Prepare me a crocodile steak and make it snappy! A crocodile steak has almost no fat and contains a central bone. When char-grilled, it has a similar colour and flavour to pork but a texture similar to tuna.

Slightly Gum-Smoked Crocodile
- 1 crocodile steak per person
- Freshly ground peppercorns
- Lemon aspen or lime juice to cover steaks
- Gum or tea tree branches

Method: To cook crocodile steaks, start by heating a grilling a pan over gum or tea tree branches that are burning hot. Rub the steaks with some juice and sprinkle pepper on them. Put the steaks on the grill and turn them a few times until they are cooked to medium rare.

YABBIES & CRAYFISH

YABBIES

This is undoubtedly my favourite Bush Tucker - more flavourful and tender than lobster and so easy to catch and cook. Crayfish and marron are very similar. Yabbies are freshwater crayfish and prawn-like crustaceans that can be found in both fresh and salt water. These creatures grow up to about 15 cm and burrow in estuaries. After their hibernation period, they emerge to spawn and shed their shell. Yabbies can be found in sand, dams, lakes, and creeks. They have the shape of a lobster but the size of a king prawn, with one claw being more prominent in males. Red claw is an introduced species, and there are no bag limits or restrictions on how many of them you can catch. If yabbies are caught in muddy streams, they must be soaked overnight. It's best to keep yabbies alive in water until they are cooked, as their flesh deteriorates quickly when dead. Salt must be added to the water that yabbies are boiled in. You can tell when they are cooked because their exoskeletal shell turns orange/red.

Yabbie Cooking

Method: Fill a large container with water and bring it to a boil. Add ½ kg salt to 10 litres of water and stir it well. Put the yabbies in the boiling water and cook for 3 minutes. Next, remove the pan from the heat and let the yabbies cool in the water. This will help retain their moisture and give the best taste. Once cooled, drain the water and enjoy your delicious yabbies!

Yabbies Served on Gum Leaves

- 24 yabbies

Sauce
- 600ml water
- 2 heaped tbsp powdered milk
- 1 tbsp flour
- 2 eggs
- salt and pepper to taste

Method: To cook and clean yabbies, remove their tails and shells. Place the yabbies in a pie dish or a camp oven. To make the sauce, mix powdered milk and flour in a container with a bit of cold water until you have a thick mixture that can be poured. Place the saucepan on coals with water and bring it to a boil. Remove it from the heat and add the milk mixture, stirring until it becomes creamy. Add the beaten egg, salt, and pepper, and stir well. Pour this sauce over the yabbies in the camp oven. Heat through for 30 minutes to an hour. It's a pity that yabbies are sometimes used for fishing bait; what a waste!

Skewered Yabbies
Many people carry smoked bacon in their packs. Apart from using it at breakfast, with eggs, yabbies, and bacon for lunch, is excellent!
- 24 large yabbie tails, shelled and washed
- 6 bacon rashers
- Bamboo or metal skewers

Method: Cut the bacon into strips and then half each strip lengthwise. Wrap each yabbie tail with a bacon strip, then place them on a skewer. Grill the skewered yabbies over hot coals for approximately ten minutes. Add bush tomatoes, onions, and fresh green vegetables to the skewer for a more fulfilling meal. Enjoy!

CRAYFISH
Crayfish and lobster are names used to describe the sea crayfish in Australia, such as the rock lobster caught in Australian waters. The freshwater crayfish species include marron, yabbies, and the Murray River crayfish. If you are wandering around the Murray and Murrumbidgee rivers of New South Wales and Victoria, and the streams are clear, you may spot some Murray crays, which are about 30 cm long and can weigh up to one kilogram. The Murray River variety has an unusual blue-black body with cream claws, and the body and claws are white-tipped.

If you throw a line with a fish or meat bait, you can coax them into your landing net. To ensure freshness and excellent flavour and texture, it's best to kill these crustaceans just before cooking them. If you spot one, it's an excellent opportunity to test your fishing skills, and the reward will be delectable.

Char-Grilled Crayfish
- 1 fresh Murray River crayfish
- ½ pannikin oil (butter is better but melts in backpacks!)
- ½ pannikin native lime or lemon juice
- Native peppercorns and salt

Method: To prepare grilled lobster, heat the grill over hot coals. Next, break the lobster in half and split the tail down the centre. Mix all the ingredients thoroughly. Baste the crayfish with the mixture and place the shell on the grill. Cook for four minutes, then turn and cook the meat side for two minutes. Baste again and repeat the procedure for about 15-20 minutes. Once cooked, the crayfish meat will be white and mouthwatering.

MARRON
Marron is an Australian freshwater crayfish commonly found in southwest Western Australia, where they are farmed for gourmet eating nationally

and internationally. A non-native marron variety, red claw, is also found in Queensland waters. Although similar to yabbies, marron can be distinguished by the five ridges on the back of their head and a pair of centre spines on their tail fan. Once only found in the large and permanent freshwater pools of coastal streams, marron can now be found in man-made water systems. However, unlike native species, they have difficulty surviving when ponds dry up during summer. Marron's reddish shell is shed many times in the first few years of its life. They hide during the daylight hours and emerge at sunset, making it best to set traps for harvesting the next day. If camping near a freshwater pool, you can use a piece of fish or meat on a line to coax the marron and net them by hand. Always have hot coals and a camp oven ready for boiling, shelling, and enjoying these tasty treats.

Marron Nibbles
- Marrons, as many as required per person
- Water
- White wine, if available
- Native peppercorns
- Salt

Method: Place a camp oven on hot coals and bring water to a boil. Add wine, peppercorns, and salt, and then add the marrons. Allow the mixture to simmer for approximately two minutes until the marron shells turn bright red. Remove the marrons and dunk them in cold water. Once they have cooled down, twist the body from the head and enjoy the deliciously flavoured meat.

POULTRY

EMU

The emu is a large, flightless bird native to Australia. It has an ostrich-like body and dark plumage. Emus cannot fly, but they lay the largest edible eggs in the world. One emu egg is equivalent to about seven hen eggs. They can run fast and outrun a car for a short distance. Emus are the closest living relative to the Tyrannosaurus Rex but are primarily friendly unless provoked. If angered, they can kick you to death and disembowel you with their long, powerful claws on their legs. They are compulsive thieves and will try to swallow anything they can pick up with their mouths. Australia is the only country commercially exporting meat from its national emblems, the kangaroo and emu. Since emus can overbreed in certain areas and become pests because they eat crops and break down fences, farmed birds and fertilised eggs are sold to Australian farmers, expanding this industry. The emu's hide is tanned commercially, and its fat is made into emu oil, which is extracted and used as a natural painkiller that hastens healing. Emu meat regulations vary from state to state, and the emu's lean red meat is classified as poultry. It is high in protein and iron and has a gamey flavour with a sweet aftertaste. A hindquarter of emu can be roasted or sliced into steaks. Fillets of emu cooked on a grill over hot coals are very tasty, and smoked or char-grilled slithers of emu are popular. Emu meat is reasonably priced and still exported to many countries.

Barbecued Emu
- 1 young male emu

Method: Place the emu on hot coals in a decent-sized hole and cover it with gum or green branches. Cook it until the feathers have disappeared and the skin turns golden brown. After that, use mallee (green) roots to rub and remove the quills. Finally, serve it on tin plates. This is a genuine Australian bush food delicacy.

Emu Egg Scramble
- 1 emu egg
- ¼ pannikin cream
- Gob of butter
- Salt & pepper

Method: To prepare a green emu egg, make small holes on both ends of the egg. Cover one hole with your finger and insert a skewer through the other hole to scramble the yolk. Blow gently through the uncovered hole to empty the egg into a bowl. Whisk the egg with cream, salt, and pepper. Melt some butter in a frypan on your campfire. Pour the egg mixture into the frypan and stir until cooked. Serve hot with a slice of damper.

AUSSIE BREAD

DAMPER

is a type of bush bread cooked on an open fire in Australia. The best part about making damper or bread in the bush is that you don't have to use precise measurements for your ingredients as long as you allow it to rise. You can also add a variety of ingredients that you can find in the bush, such as native peppercorns, lemon myrtle leaves, Macadamia nuts, or pulped Bogong moths.

Basic Damper
- 2 pannikins (tin cups), self-raising flour
- ½ teaspoon salt:
- 250 gms butter
- Milk

Method: First, sift flour and salt and then rub in butter. Mix in enough milk to make a non-sticky dough. Allow it to sit while the sides and bottom of the camp oven are floured. Then, put the camp oven on hot coals and place the dough in the oven. Cook for about half an hour. The damper is cooked when it sounds hollow inside when tapped.

Aussie Beer Bread
- 3 pannikins self-raising flour
- ½ pannikin sugar
- 1 pinch salt
- 1 can beer

Method: You need beer instead of yeast to make delicious bread. First, ensure your hot coals have settled and prepare your camp oven. Mix all the ingredients until they form a semi-dry dough, then put the dough in the greased camp oven. Cook for about 30-40 minutes. Once it's cooked, take a clean gum leaf, spread some butter over the bread, pull it apart and start eating!

Lemonade Scones
Lemonade scones are a great treat for children, especially when you're out camping. The recipe is simple enough for them to assist you in making it. All you need is a tin of lemonade, butter, and jam. These scones will satisfy the kids and keep them content, and they may even please some of the adults as well.
- 2 pannikins self-raising flour
- 1 pinch salt
- 1 can lemonade
- Butter

Method: To prepare your camp oven, spread butter on the bottom and sides of it. Then, coat the greased camp oven with a layer of flour to prevent the dough from sticking and burning. Ensure your hot coals have settled and your camp oven is ready. Mix all the ingredients until you form a semi-dry dough. Add more flour if the dough is too wet, but do not make it too dry. Divide the dough into 6 to 8 smaller pieces and place them in the camp oven, ensuring they are not touching. Even if they expand and move together, don't worry; they will cook initially before joining. Cook for 20-30 minutes. Once cooked, take a clean leaf, spread jam, cream, honey or any other topping over the scones, pull them apart and start eating while they are still warm.

RED MEAT

BUFFALO

Water buffaloes were introduced to Australia by Asian immigrants as labour animals for farming. They are called "water" buffaloes because they love soaking in water and can often be found near rivers and deep creeks. These animals also produce milk. For many years, many water buffaloes roamed freely throughout the Northern Territory. However, as feral animals, their hard hooves have caused environmental damage, and no hunting limits have been placed on them. Feral buffalos have a significant impact on the environment. They cause soil erosion, channel floodwaters, and increase saltwater intrusion into freshwater habitats. This results in the destruction of wetland vegetation, which leads to the decline of native species and loss of habitat for waterbirds. They also spread disease to farm cattle. Feral buffalos were eliminated from Kakadu National Park and the northern wetlands via an extensive eradication program involving expert shooters in culling from helicopters. The program successfully reduced their numbers, but complete eradication was impossible due to their continuous multiplication and spread.

Bodybuilders now recognise the benefits of low-fat, high-protein meat obtained from buffalo. As a result, farmed buffalo meat is now in demand locally and internationally. If you want to add them to your bush tucker menu, you can help Australia's ecosystem by removing them from it. Older water buffaloes have darker meat than beef, while younger meat is lighter pink. The easiest way to prepare and eat water buffalo meat is to treat it as another form of beef with a gamey flavour. You can substitute beef bought from the butcher in any of these recipes. Prime buffalo cuts such as steak and eye fillet are the most tender and similar in size to beef.

Rough Red Buffalo Steaks
- 1 × 2.5 cm buffalo steak per person - 2.5 cm thick
- A rough red wine
- Local native herbs
- Animal fat or oil

Method: Marinating buffalo meat overnight is a good idea for a delightful taste. To do so, cover the steaks with red wine, local herbs, and some oil (if you have it). Turn the steaks a few times during the marination process. An hour before eating, prepare a fire. Once the coals are hot, heat a pan by hanging it over the coals. Melt some fat or oil in the pan before cooking. Place the steaks in the pan and grill for a few minutes before turning. Add some of the marinades to the pan and grill for about five minutes before turning again and repeating the process. At this point, the buffalo steaks should be medium-rare. Serve the steaks on tin plates. To enhance the flavour, quickly reduce any leftover marinade and pour it over the buffalo. Enjoy this delicious meal with a cup of local mint or herb tea.

Hot Coal Steaks with Native Peppercorns
- 1 steak for each person
- A few small branches of native peppercorns

Method: After a long day in the wilderness, a campfire is essential to recharge. Adding peppercorn branches to hot coals and layering on the steaks requires minimal effort and boosts energy levels.

Aussie Shovel Burgers
Nowadays, most campers come equipped with versatile utensils, but did you know that a shovel can be used as a grill plate?
- A quantity of finely chopped meat
- 1½ pannikin (tin cup) flour
- ½ pannikin soaked damper crumbs
- 1 egg
- A sprinkling of dried onion flakes
- Duck fat, if available, or any lard

Method: Mix all the ingredients and shape them into patties to make delicious hamburgers. Heat some lard over hot coals on a hot plate or shovel and fry the burgers. Recent studies have shown that lard once believed to be unhealthy, is quite beneficial for your heart. Once cooked, serve the burgers on a damper scone and garnish the plate with some Warrigal spinach, if available. This is a fun experiment that results in a tasty meal.

PRESERVING MEAT IN THE BUSH
However, with any large catch, eating all of the animal fresh is only possible if you're with a large group of people. Here are a couple of easy ways to make your bush-caught meat last longer:

Smoking
One of the simplest ways to preserve meat is by suspending meat strips in the fire's heat and smoke. The fat melts out of the meat, dries it and preserves it. It's essential to allow the rendering process to drip the fat out. The less fat, the drier and meet. The drier and meet, the longer it will last. The fat dripping from the meat will also continue to fuel the fire. The smoking fire should remain hot enough to boil water. The process takes approximately 3 hours for every 1 kg of meat, regardless of the number of pieces (i.e. ten pieces of 1kg each will take only 3 hours to smoke if they are all suspended fully in the smoke and heat). The process is faster if you can do it in an enclosed space. The resulting flavour is rich and earthy, with intense aromas that bring out the meat's full flavour.

Commercially, smoked meats sell for much more than fresh meat because of their deliciousness. Many commercially prepared smokers come with wonderful recipes that you can take camping. Most people buy hickory wood chips and place their strips of meat on a grilling rack in a camp oven over the smoking wood chips. Smoked meat can last 1-2 weeks or longer if kept refrigerated.

Jerky

In the past, Indigenous stockmen prepared jerky by cutting the meat into thin strips, rubbing it with salt and/or baking soda, and laying it across the back of their saddle while droving and letting it dry out in the hot sun. Nowadays, there are many more complicated jerky recipes available.

Backyard Buffalo Jerky

- 1 1/2 kg. Buffalo Sirloin cut into strips.

Method: Cut meat into strips about ½ cm thick. Mix a 1 kg packet of salt with a packet of baking soda – thoroughly rub into all the meat. Save any leftover salt rub.

Marinade

- ⅓ tsp garlic powder
- ½ tsp pepper
- 1 tsp onion powder
- ¼ pannikin (tin cup) Worcestershire sauce
- ¼ pannikin soy sauce

Mix the ingredients and soak the meat in a sealed container. Let it marinate in the refrigerator for 4-24 hours, preferably longer. Rub the pieces with the salt rub again. The more salt you use, the more it keeps flies away. You can dust off the salt later when the meat is dry. Take out the meat and place it on racks in the sun without the pieces touching each other. Cover with a piece of mosquito netting or fine cheesecloth. This is a perfect snack for bushwalking; it is high in protein and low in fat and carbohydrates. It's an excellent energy booster and tastes delicious. Enjoy it to the fullest!

KANGAROO

Kangaroos are a beloved symbol of Australia. People love seeing them in the wild or animal parks. However, kangaroo populations can quickly become excessive, especially after a wet season. They can eat an entire landscape until it's barren, and then they begin to starve. Female kangaroos can have multiple embryos that remain dormant until there is adequate food for the joey to grow. When it rains, the kangaroo population can explode. Farmers are issued permits to shoot kangaroos on their property when they need to be culled. Instead of wasting the meat, it's an excellent opportunity for campers to try wild-caught kangaroo. The flavour is rich and complete, and the meat is fresh from the field to the plate. Kangaroo fur has been sold commercially for some time, but kangaroo meat has only recently been marketed internationally. However, indigenous Australians have hunted and eaten kangaroo meat for thousands of years. Kangaroos were hunted by stalking, spearing, trapping, or driving them into traps. Some stories even tell of kangaroos being chased until they dropped. South Australia was the first state to establish a legal processing plant for kangaroo meat. Other states are gradually recognising the value of this animal product. The whole animal should be used rather than leaving a culled animal to rot in a paddock. Kangaroo hindquarter cuts include the saddle, porterhouse steak, fillet, tail, and minced meat. Cook kangaroo meat slowly. Its flesh is dark red and has one of the lowest cholesterol levels of all red meats. Organic kangaroo meat has become popular with the keto and bodybuilding population. Kangaroo meat's texture is similar to beef, and its flavour is slightly more robust. Many Australian bushmen carry enough provisions to cook kangaroo in a variety of ways, such as kangaroo tail soup, braised kangaroo tail, roasted leg of kangaroo, kangaroo rissoles, kangaroo stew, or barbecued fillet.

Kangaroo Tail Soup
This recipe requires an early start. The three-hour cooking time provides ample time to enjoy nature before enjoying the soup.
- 6 joints of kangaroo tail
- Water
- 1 cup split peas
- 2 onions
- Dried noodles; macaroni or spaghetti
- Any vegetables you may have, fresh, tinned or dried
- Salt and pepper to taste

Method: To prepare this dish, start by heating an empty camp oven on a bed of coals. Once the oven is hot, add a jointed kangaroo tail to it. Cover the kangaroo's tail with water and bring it to a boil. Then, add split peas, onions and noodles to the boiling water. Boil everything until all the ingredients, including the meat, are cooked. Next, add the diced vegetables and cook until they are tender. Finally, add salt and pepper to taste. This recipe should serve between 6 to 8 people.

Roasted Kangaroo Leg
You can serve this dish to anyone, rich or poor, and they'll keep hopping back for more.
- 1 kangaroo leg
- 1 cup dripping

- Stuffing
- ½ loaf bread
- 1 large onion, chopped finely
- 2 strips bacon, chopped finely
- 2 soft tomatoes, chopped finely
- 1 dessertspoon mixed herbs
- 1 egg
- Salt and pepper to taste

Method: First, take the kangaroo leg and cut deep pockets into it to hold the stuffing. For the stuffing, remove the crust from the bread and crumb it. Then, add the bacon, onion, and tomatoes. Mix everything with the breadcrumbs, and add the egg, herbs, salt, and pepper—stuff this mixture into the pockets of the kangaroo leg. Next, bake the kangaroo leg in a camp oven with the dripping for 2½-3 hours until it is well cooked. Make sure to bake the meat with the dripping because it has no fat.

Kangaroo Rissoles

This recipe requires a bushman's pack with onions, potatoes, eggs, and tomato sauce, an Australian favourite.
- 1 kg kangaroo meat
- 2 onions
- 2 potatoes
- 1 egg
- tomato sauce
- salt and pepper

Method: Chop the meat, onions, and potatoes into small pieces or mince them. Then, add salt and pepper to the mixture and stir in an egg to bind the ingredients together. Shape the mixture into balls and place them in a camp oven. Add a dessertspoonful of tomato sauce to each ball, and bake slowly.

RABBITS

In Australia, the colonial English introduced rabbits and foxes for recreational hunting, believing that they would keep each other under control. However, their populations exploded, causing devastation to the native flora and fauna. Due to their hormones, fox meat is not considered suitable for eating as it smells unpleasant. However, rabbit meat is beautiful. Rabbits helped many small Australian bush communities survive the great depression. In the 1950s, Australia was overrun with rabbits and hares, and a rabbit-proof fence, three times longer than the Great Wall of China, was built to divide the country. Nowadays, targeted hunting and the introduction of the myxomatosis virus have brought rabbit populations under control. However, owning rabbits is still illegal in Queensland due to their potential danger to the environment and economy. Although rabbit meat is farmed in New South Wales, wild-caught rabbit meat is also easily acquired during camping trips. Rabbit meat is convenient to cook and can be prepared in various ways, such as stewed with Warrigal greens or roasted to one's liking. My husband likes to make a dish he calls…

Kentucky Fried Rabbit
My husband cooks this at a farmhouse when he goes away hunting. It could also be prepared and taken on a camping trip, ready to be deep-fried in the camp oven on the first night.
- 1 or 2 cleaned rabbits cut into six pieces each
- Salt & Vinegar & 1 litre water made into a brine
- 1 Cup Flour
- 1 Egg
- Mixed herbs = (The Colonel's secret recipe is Basil, Thyme, Origano, Dried Mustard, Ground Ginger, Paprika, Garlic, Onion Powder, Celery Salt, White Pepper, & Black Pepper) You add whichever herbs float your boat.
- Breadcrumbs
- 1 litre cooking oil
- More Salt and pepper to taste

Method: To prepare this rabbit dish, make a brine and soak the meat in it overnight. This process will turn the meat white and remove most of its gamey taste. After soaking, microwave the meat for 20 minutes or dry it in a heated camp oven. Once the meat has cooled, roll it in egg, flour, breadcrumbs, and mixed herbs. You can repeat this process to make the coating extra crispy and thick. Finally, deep fry the meat for 15-20 minutes and serve it with Warrigal greens and mashed Bunya nuts (or mashed potatoes). Yummy!

SMALLER THINGS

BOGONG MOTHS

Indigenous communities in the Australian Alps of New South Wales and across a large area of Victoria considered Bogong moths as one of their staple foods due to their tastiness and nutritional value. These moths would gather in rock caverns during the summer, and that was when they were collected for a feast. Interestingly, if you were blindfolded and someone offered you a roasted Bogong moth, you would likely mistake it for a giant peanut.

Coolamon Moth Nuts

- 1 coolamon
- A quantity of Bogong moths

Method: In Australia, Bogong moths often plague the region. During such times, the moths can be caught, cleaned, and frozen for future cooking. "Coolamon" is derived from the Wiradjuric language, which refers to a multi-purpose shallow vessel or dish with curved sides. These vessels are similar in shape to a canoe and range in length from 30 to 70 cm. Indigenous women traditionally used coolamons to carry water, fruit, nuts and cradle babies. If a coolamon is unavailable, moths can be placed in a pan or an appropriate dish. To cook the moths, place several live coals on top of a coolamon full of moths and gently mix. When the coals cool, replace them with hot coals and continue until the moths are warmed and debris rubs off. The cooked moths have an oily-nutty flavour that is enhanced during cooking.

Macadamia Pop

Sitting around a campfire and having your camp oven popping moths and roasting macadamias is very satisfying.

- Some macadamia nut oil
- A handful of macadamia nuts with husks removed
- A handful of Bogong moths, optional

Method: Place the camp oven on hot coals and heat macadamia oil. Add macadamia nuts and moths, then shake them around the oven until roasted. The moths will dry and taste like peanuts, while the macadamia nuts will be delicious.

WITCHETTY GRUBS

A witchetty grub is an edible caterpillar of an Australian moth that bores into various species of wattle. The word "witchetty" refers to two particular types of wattles. To cook the grub, you can wash it and grill it on a hot plate until it has a crispy skin and soft flesh, similar to the crispy fat on the back of a lamb chop. If you're in the bush, look for old-looking wattle trees without leaves and check the underground roots for the grubs. You'll know you've found one when you see cracked soil above its living quarters. Nowadays, there are many recipes for witchery grubs, ranging from cheese dip to soup.

Witchetty Soup
- 10 fresh witchetty grubs
- 40 ml oil
- Dried onions
- 1-litre stock
- Native peppercorns
- Salt
- ½ pannikin (tin cup) powdered milk, made fairly thickly
- a little flour

Method: This recipe is enough for two servings. First, heat a saucepan on hot coals and slowly sauté the grubs in oil. Add stock, dried onions, peppercorns, and salt. Cook the mixture for 1& 1/2 hours. Then, add thickened milk. To thicken the soup, make a paste by mixing a little water with flour and pour it into the soup. Stir until it thickens slightly.

HONEY ANTS
Honey ants, known as Camponotus inflatus, are found in Western Australia and the Northern Territory desert areas. These ants have specialised workers who are force-fed till their abdomens swell enormously. Other ants then extract nourishment from them through the process of trophallaxis. They serve as living larders. According to researchers, the honey these ants produce has antibacterial and anti-fungal properties, confirming Indigenous knowledge. The Australian honey ant has been used as a bush food and in traditional medicine by indigenous people for thousands of years to treat colds and sore throats. By analysing the properties of the honey, Australian researchers have discovered that it is highly effective against Staphylococcus aureus bacteria, commonly known as golden staph. This honey is a precious resource and has a lot of cultural significance to Indigenous people.

Honey Ant Bubble Tea
Once extracted from their nests, they are a great snack by simply biting off the abdomen from the head and thorax. They can be used as garnishes on other sweets, as a substitute for a cherry on top. They are great in cocktails and a taste sensation when you put them in tea or beer.

CAMP OVEN COOKING

These days, cooking over the open fire in the bush has been enhanced by using a camp oven, a heavy cast-iron cooking pot. They are simple to use, easy to clean, and a great way to increase the iron in your diet. Always make a good fire with plenty of coals, especially when cooking. Mulga wood is an excellent choice as it provides long-lasting coals. However, pine bought in firewood packets may flare up and burn quickly, leaving few coals. Fortunately, camp oven cooking doesn't require many coals. Place some on the lid and stand it on them to cook most dishes.

It's essential to preheat the camp oven on the central fire so that it already has enough heat when placed on the coals.

When you need all-around heat for foods like bread, pastries, and cakes, heat the lid on the fire until it's hot enough, then place it in the camp oven for immediate heat.

If it starts raining while you're cooking, cover the top of the oven with the blade of a shovel or a piece of corrugated tin to prevent rain from cooling it down.

CAMP OVEN CARE
Never pour cold water into a hot camp oven. The oven will crack. When washing it, always use hot or warm water. After washing, rub inside and out with oil or fat. This will prevent your oven from rusting.

PAPER TEST FOR OVEN TEMPERATURE
Place a piece of white paper inside the oven to find out the oven temperature without the need for a thermostat:

Temperature	Farenheit	Centigrade	Paper Test
Too Hot			Black & On Fire
Very Hot Oven	500	260	Dark Brown
Hot Oven	375-400	200	Light Brown
Moderate Oven	325-375	170	Yellow
Slow Oven	250-325	120	Crust

INDIGENOUS WORDS & LANGUAGE

The Indigenous languages are dying out. Indigenous language was a rapidly evolving and changing thing. The Western concept of making words stay, of correct spelling and syntax and preserving language has slowed this process. These languages are not as dynamic or vital as they once were because of the methods used in an attempt to preserve them. The rapid evolution of these languages happened for two main reasons.

1) In many mobs, the prohibition against speaking the name of a dead member meant that if the individual were named for any commonly used word like "Kangaroo" (or any of the things listed here), a new word would have to be invented to substitute for the word used as a given name. This means that by the time we have catalogued and categorised the words, they would have all morphed into new ones. Forcing the languages to stay frozen in time is also a massive break from cultural traditions.

2) Secondly, because of the importance of conversation and debate within small nomadic groups (one runs out of gossip quickly in small groups), the ability to invent and discuss philosophical concepts was highly prized, resulting in complex and philosophical languages that cannot be translated as a single word for a concept. Additionally, the concept itself may not exist within any other language. New vocabulary and interesting concepts were sorted and exchanged at any large gathering of the tribes to be brought back to and discussed during the year's travels by the smaller mobs.

Thus, these languages grew, evolved, cross-pollinated and produced beautiful new seeds and ever-flourishing cultural concepts.

Once, many hundreds of distinct languages were used by the many indigenous language groups here in Australia. Many of these have died out. Today, only 247 of these remain, and most of these are only partial. Attempts are being made to record, preserve and teach these languages to the new generations of each culture before those who still speak them die out. Below are some Macquarie Dictionary preserved and recorded words that have become commonly used among indigenous language groups, although each mob will have its distinct terminologies.

BODY PARTS

Banarang	Blood	Garaga	Mouth
Barangal	Throat	Garungan	Fingernail
Barrang	Belly	Gidigidi	Armpit
Barrangal	Skin	Gumirri	Vagina
Biba	Rib	Gunat	Matted Hair
Budbut	Heart	Guni	Faeces, Shit
Bugai	Fat (Human)	Guri	Ear
Bunang Guruk	Knee	Mai	Eye
Bung	Buttocks	Manuwi	Foot
Bura	Testicles	Marbal	Chest
Dalang	Tongue	Midyung	Sor
Damara	Hand	Nabang	Breast
Dara	Tooth	Naga	Liver
Darra	Leg, Thigh	Ngulun	Forehead
Djarrung	Shoulder	Nuga	Nose
Djiwaxra	Hair	Una	Elbow
Dyara	Bone	Walu	Shin
Gabara	Head	Wiling	Lips
Gadlyang	Nape, Neck	Yarring	Beard
Gadya	Penis	Yilabil	Urine, Piss
Galgala	Smallpox		

KIN RELATIONSHIPS

Babana	Brother	Guman	Grandfather
Biyanga	Father	Guwalgalyung	Elder Sister
Damali	Namesake	Guwalgang	Elder Brother
Djambing	Sister-in-Law	Mubi	Mourner at Funeral
Djurumin	Sister	Mugung	Lover
Durung	son	Mugungalyi	Marital Partner
Duruninang	Daughter	Mulamang	Husband
Dyinmang	Wife	Ngalaiya	Ally
Gabami	Intermediary	Ngaramada	Younger Brother
Gamarada	Friend, Comrade	Ngarangalyung	Younger Sister
Gulang	Widow in Mourning	Wiyanga	Mother

HUMAN CLASSIFICATIONS

Dyin	Woman	Man	Fisherwoman
Dyinuragang	Old Woman	Man	(Also Ghost)
Gaiyanaiyung	Old Man	Mani	Fisherman
Gaiyara	Name	Mula	Man
Garadyigan	Doctor	Waruwi	Girl
Guragalung	Young Man	Wawura	Rascal Female
Guragalungalyung	Young Woman	Wungarra	Boy
Gurung	Child, Baby	Yura	Person
Maiyal	Stranger		

LANGUAGE, MYTHOLOGY, CEREMONY

Biyani	Curative Operation Performed by Women To Cure Illness in Other Women	Nanga Mai	Dream
		Nanung	Piercing of the Nasal Septum To Receive a Bone or Reed Decoration
Buduwai	Ritual for Preventing Children From Becoming Thieves by Scorching Their Fingers	Yabun	Music Made by Singing and Beating Time
Djanaba	Laughter	Yalabi or Daiyalung or Bora	Ceremony
Gaxabara	a Dance		
Malgun	Woman With Two Joints of the Little Finger on her Left Hand Removed Ritually	Yulang or Yirabadjang	Tooth Extraction Initiation Ceremony for Young Men
Man	Ghost		

FOOD, COOKING AND FIRE

Djarraba	Firestick: Gun	Gili	Flame, Light
Gadial	Smoke	Guwiyang	Fire
Ganalang Or Yuruga	Heat	Ngarrun Nggununy Or Badalya	Fat of Meat Food
Garuma	Blubber		

PIECES OF EQUIPMENT

Aragung	Shield for war (Large & Solid)
Bangada	Ornaments
Bangala	Water-carrying vessel made from bark tied at each end
Barra	Fishhook
Barrin	Apron-style covering worn by un-married girls made from spun possum hair tied in cords from a possum-hair belt
Budbili	Possum Rug
Bumarit Or Wumarang or Bumarang	Boomerang for fighting
Damang	Cap
Darral	Feather Head Ornament
Duwal	Spear (short, with two barbs)
Galarra	Fish Harpoon (5-7m, with 4 barbs)
Gamai	Spear
Garradjun	Fishing line made from bark
Gulima	Basket made from the knot of a tree
Gunang	Spear for hand-to-hand combat
Guni	Yamstick
Gunya	Dwelling made by people
Guwariya	Fish harpoon for children
Muding	Sm Fish Harpoon
Mugu	Stone Hatchet
Narawang	Paddle, Oar
Ngalangala	Club with a mushroom-shaped head
Ngamul	Sinker for a fishing line made from a small stone
Ngurra	Camp
Nuwi	Canoe
Wigun	Spear thrower made from heavy wood with one end rounded to be used as a digging stick.
Wuda, Wudi	Club shaped from a long piece of wood thicker at one end
Wumara	Spear thrower about one metre long, with a shell scraper at one end made from a gadyan (Sydney Cockel)
Yalga	Barb of a spear
Yung	Shield for parrying

LANDSCAPE

Bulga	Hill	Gumirri	Hole
Buruwang	Island	Guru	Deep Water
Dyiral	Shoal	Marrang	Sand, Beach
Ganing	Cave	Muru	Road, Path
Garagula	Ebb Tide	Nura	Country, Place
Garrigarrang	Sea		

NATURAL ITEMS

Badu	Water	Giba	Stone
Bamal	Earth	Gura	Wind
Barabung Or		Gurbuny	Fog
Minyimulung	Dew	Guwara	High Wind
Baragula	Flood Tide	Guwing	Sun
Birrung	Star	Marri Yanada	Full Moon
Buduwangung	Magellanic Clouds	Mungi	Lightning
Burra, Garrayura	Sky	Murungal	Thunder
Danagal	Ice	Walan, Bana	Rain
Duruga	Falling Star	Warriwul	Milky Way
Garaguru	Cloud	Yanada	Moon

REPTILES

Bayagin	Leaf-Tailed Gecko	Malya,	Diamond Python
Daning	Death Adder	Ngarrang	Bearded Dragon
Gan	Reptiles (snake, goanna or lizard)	Wirragadar	Bandy-Bandy

LOCAL ANIMALS

Badagarang	Grey Kangaroo	Marriyagang	Tiger Cat
Banggarai	Swamp Wallaby	Mirrin	Marsupial Mouse
Buduru	Potoroo	Wanyuwa	Horse
Bugul, Wurra	Mouse, Rat	Wirambi	Bat
Bungu	Flying Phalanger	Wiring	Female Animals
Burumin	Possum	Wubin	Feather-Tail or Pygmy Glider
Dingu	Dingo	Wulaba	Rock Wallaby
Djubi	Sugar Glider	Wularu	Wallaroo
Dun	Tail	Wumbat	Wombat
Ganimung	Rat-Kangaroo		

BIRDS

Binit	Tawny Frogmouth	Guma	King Parrot
Binyang	Bird	Guriyal	Parrot, Parrakeet
Bubuk	Boobook Owl	Guwali	Shag, Cormorant
Buming	Redbill	Marrigang	Sittella
Bunda	Hawk	Mulgu	Black Swan
Bunyarinarin	Masked Lapwing	Munu.	Bill
Burumurring	Wdg-Tailed Eagle	Murradjulbi	Singing Bushlark
Diamuldiamul	Whistling Kite	Muruduwin	Fairy Wren
Dyaramak	Sacred Kingfisher	Ngunyul	Feather
Dyuralya	Brolga	Ngurra	Birds' Nest
Gaban	Egg	Nuwalgang	Magpie Goose
Garadi	Black Cockatoo	Urwinarriwing	Eastern Curlew
Garrangabumarri	Pelican	Wangawang	Ground Parrot
Garrawi	Cockatoo	Wilbing	Wing
Girra~Girra	Seagull	Wirgan	Noisy Friarbird
Gugurruk	Black-Shld Kite	Wugan	Crow
Gulina	Night Heron	Wungawunga	Wonga Pigeon
Gulungaga	Red-Brwed Finch		

FISH & SEA LIFE

Badangi	Rock Oyster	Garuma.	Black Bream
Baludarri	Leather-Jacket	Gawura	Whale
Barung	Yellowtail Kingfish	Ginari S	Shovel-Nosed Ray
Baruwaluwu	Dolphin	Guruwin	Grey Nurse Shark
Burra	Eel	Magura	Fish
Dainya	Mud Oyster	Marumara	Zebra Fish
Dalgal	Mussel	Walamai	Snapper
Daringyan	Stingray	Walumil	Prt Jackson shark
Gadyan	Sydney Cockle	Waragal	Mackerel
Gaguni	Toadfish	Yaxa	Crab

PLANTS

Bugi	Bark	Djuraduralang	Bark used to make fishing lines
Burumarri	Brown Gum	Gadigabudyari	Christmas Bell
Buruwan	Rock Lily	Galun Stem	Grasstree
Daguba	Brush Cherry	Bracken	Gurgi
Dainun	Port Jackson fig	Ganugan	Fern Root
Daranggara	Cabbage Tree	Midiny	Vegetable (edible)
Diramu	Tree	Gulgadya	Yam
Djirang	Leaf		Grasstree

Sources: These definitions are taken from the Macquarie book of Aboriginal words. There have been some minor alterations and shortenings of descriptions.
This list of "Some Words of Sydney Aboriginal Groups" compiled by -
Les Bursill JP. AIM. B.A. M.Litt (UNE) http://users.tpg.com.au/sshists/aboriginalwords.htm

INDIGENOUS WRITTEN LANGUAGE

Message-sticks, also known as talking or "black fella letters," have been mentioned by writers on the customs of Australian indigenous, but little information has been recorded on this subject. These sticks were used to convey information from one tribe to another at a distance using symbols.

The sticks were given to the messenger to help him remember the message by connecting certain pictographs, marks, or notches cut into them, which were explained to him before he set out on his journey. Though he was given a basic introduction to deliver along with the message sticks, part of the written message was private. The recipients of the message sticks were expected to understand what was being conveyed.

These message-sticks come in different sizes, ranging from an inch and a half to eighteen inches or more. They can be elaborately carved or painted or simply a rounded piece of wood or rod cut from a tree branch or sapling. Some are even made of bark or bone. The sticks are marked in various ways, including notches, dots, strokes, curves, triangular, quadrilateral, and zigzag devices, and are made with a sharp stone, bone, or broken shell.

Message-sticks are used for various purposes, such as summoning an assemblage for war or a meeting for a celebratory corroboree. The messenger who carries the stick is usually a young man, strong and active, well-known among the tribes he visits, and somewhat familiar with their dialect. On arrival at the recipient's camp, he hands the message-stick to the person to whom he has been directed to deliver it, giving the name of the sender and explaining the meaning. Women, youths, and men can carry sticks conveying friendly messages or greetings. The bearer of a message is never molested by any mobs through whose country he may have occasion to travel while engaged in this duty, even if the people he passes are not on friendly terms with his mob. This rule is of universal prevalence among native tribes throughout the continent, and a breach of it would lead to retaliation.

Unfortunately, some Indigenous people today are trying to keep their language a secret. Doing this plays into the narrative of the organisations whom it suits for the indigenous to be portrayed as 'ignorant savages.' It is sad to see these intelligent people so easily manipulated. It is always the noisy minority that causes changes that the silent majority don't want. The majority of Indigenous would like access to their written language. Many indigenous are starting to voice their desire for their written language to be made public again. Still, a persistent few are lobbying to remove all message sticks from museums and personal collections, which does not help preserve their culture. There are very few Indigenous people left who can read the sacred language, and taking it out of circulation will lead to its extinction.

The only known attempt to categorise the indigenous hieroglyphic images on the sticks was by R. H. Mathews in 1897. He asked the Indigenous people themselves for the translation and, with their full permission, published the first and only dictionary of the Australian Indigenous written language. He explains that there is indigenous written and sign language universal to nearly all indigenous nations in Australia. Yet, most indigenous people today would only know a little about this fantastic achievement, as outlined in this document. No other continent in the world has ever had a written language that is universal to every nation upon it. This is truly unique. Alexander the Great tried to achieve this. He dangled the carrot and said that anybody who could read and write Greek could become a Greek citizen, having full citizenship rights throughout his empire. Millennia before Alexander, the Australian Indigenous, had already achieved this.

R. H. Mathews explained that the message on the stick was not only what was written on it but also the timber's shape, size, and thickness. The message could differ significantly depending on the type of wood that the message sticks were made from. For example, a notched stick had a very different meaning than one that was just round on the outside. The number of notches indicates the number of people to whom the message stick must be given directly. Here is a table that summarises and simplifies R. H. Mathews's findings.

(Fig 1 and Fig 2 diagrams of message stick with labels a–k)	This is a message from a head-man of the Culgoa tribe, to the head-man of the Tinanburra tribe. The stick was handed to the messenger, at Goodooga, on the Bokhara river, New South Wales, who conveyed it to Tinanburra, on the Cuttaburra river, Queensland, the distance between the two places being about 100 miles.

When delivering the stick the messenger would supply the names of the sender, any other messengers who's has the message stick passed through, the recipient, and any information that was missing like the intention of the corrobbery.
The devices on the stick as follows: |
(map diagram)	Directions-like a mud map, drawing in the ground – where the messengers from – where the missing shirt is telling them, the corrobbery will be held. Like a letter with a sending and recieving address. Dispatched from the Bokhara river via the Birie (d), the Culgoa (e), and Cudnappa (f) rivers. The 2 mobs are meting at the Cudnappa river .
(crescent moon symbol)	The message stick was dispatched at new moon
(full moon symbol)	The mob are expected to be there by full moon
(figure of painted person)	The sender all painted up indicating to get ready for ceremony
(figure of person)	1st Messanger
(two figures)	2nd Messenger to stay with receiver until the Coroberee

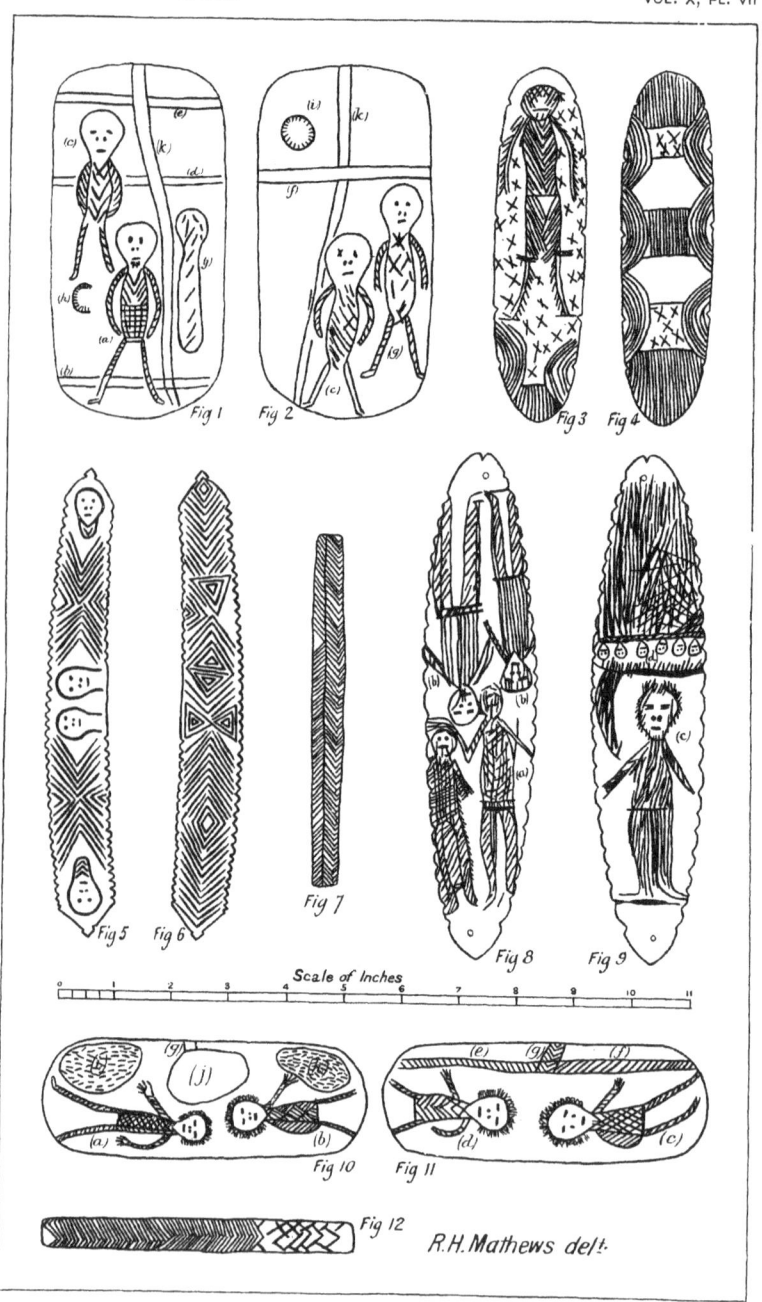

AUSTRALIAN MESSAGE-STICKS

R. H. Matthews describes it this way:

> "Figures 1 and 2.-The message-stick here represented is made of the wood of the cuttibundi tree, known to white men as quinine or Peruvian bark. Its length is six inches and an eighth, its breadth a little over three inches, and its thickness slightly exceeding three-eighths of an inch. This is a message from Nanee, Kumbo Kangaroo, a head-man of the Culgoa tribe, to Belay, Kubbi Iguana, one of the head-men of the Tinanburra tribe. Nanee handed the stick to a black fella named Imball, Kubbi Iguana, at Goodooga, on the Bokhara River, New South Wales, who conveyed it to Belay at Tinanburra, on the Cuttaburra River, Queensland, the distance between the two places being about 100 miles. When handing the stick to Belay, Imball told him that Nanee and his tribe wished to meet him (Belay) and his tribe on the Cudnappa river for the purpose of holding a corroboree. further explained to Belay the Imnball devices on the stick as follows, which will be better understood by referring to plate vI: Nanee (a) sent the message from the Bokhara river (b), by the hand of Imball (c), via the Birie (d), the Culgoa (e), and Cudnappa (f) rivers, to Belay (g); that the stick was dispatched at new moon (h), and Belay and his tribe are expected to be at Cudnappa river (f) at full moon (i); (j) represents a corroboree ground, and Belay understands from it that Nanee and his tribe are corroboreeing at the Bokhara river, which is their taorai, and, further, that on the meeting of the two tribes at full moon on the Cudnappa river a big corroboree will be held. The messenger, Imball, is shown standing beside Belay, which conveys the meaning that he will remain with the latter until he and his tribe are ready to start for the place of meeting, and that he, the messenger, will accompany them thither. The route taken by Imball in going from Goodooga to Tinanburra is shown at (k). From Belay's knowledge of the distance from the Bokhara river to the place of meeting on the Cudnappa river, he would know that the Culgoa tribe would require to start for the Bokhara very soon after he received the message at Tinanburra. Nanee and his tribe would have to travel about 70 miles and Belay and his tribe about 30 miles to reach the place of meeting."

The chevrons and swirls in Figures 3,4,5 & 6 indicate the mobs who sent the message. Each Mob would have its own markings in a similar way that every clan in Scotland has its own tartan. The individuals painted on the stick indicate who sent the messages.

Figure 7 is a small but important message stick. This herringbone pattern around the central line means to bring gifts. The fancier, the better.

Figures 8 and 9 are letters telling the recipient to expect guests. They are very polite. The front side indicates that a man and his wife are bringing two other people. Four travellers altogether. They will arrive at the Mob of the headman pictured on the back with all his people around him. The notches indicate the estimated time of travel. Approximately two months – so be expecting them.

Figures 10 and 11 depict the headmen of two mobs. The circles beside them indicate their campsites. The black circle in the middle is a campsite where the two mobs will meet. The back suggests the road to travel. The diagonal lines indicate footsteps. The message on the back is the critical message. It tells the mob to watch for the footsteps leading off the side of the road to indicate where this campsite will be hidden. If either MOB arrives there, first, they are to follow the footsteps to the hidden campsite.

Figure 12 is lovely. It is a short, circular stick with a simple message. It was sent to Billy, a worker on a cattle station in central Queensland, asking him to bring his family to a big Corroboree of many mobs and to bring gifts.

As we can see from these message sticks, they vary mundane topics through notices of large gatherings. This shows that this style of writing was accessible to all indigenous people and was not something that was kept secret to only a few. These messages are often delivered to Indigenous individuals surrounded by non-Indigenous people. And the messages were discussed and not hidden from them. It is time to restore this beautiful form of communication to its traditional practitioners.

PROTO-WRITING CORRELATES TO INDIGENOUS CAVE "ART"
In 2023, the academic community finally acknowledged the deciphering of numerous cave paintings in Europe as Proto-Writing. These marks were decoded by an amateur archaeologist named Ben Bacon. During the Ice Age, hunter-gatherers in Europe used cave drawings to record detailed information about the animals around them. The markings in over 600 Ice Age images across Europe reveal a record of information and references to a calendar. The dots, shapes, and other markings appear alongside depictions of various species, such as reindeer, wild horses, fish, bison, and extinct cattle called aurochs. For instance, a "Y" sign, formed by adding a diverging line to another, meant "giving birth." The team determined that the number of marks was a record, by lunar

months, of when the animals were breeding by using the birth cycles of equivalent animals today as a reference.

We love our academic community. By and large, they are selfless seekers of truth. They have and will continue to guard and serve humanity's best interests. However, established academics are taught to stay well within the bounds of what they have read. They have seen the consequences of what happens to their colleagues if they stray too far from the accepted norm. It then necessarily falls to "amateur" archaeologists to push the bounds of the known outside of established academia. Even when this takes a terrible toll upon them, they become labelled as "fringe archaeologists" and derided. Their lives and careers can be destroyed because of these labels. Yet, after their death, their findings are often proven. Don Marcelino Sanz de Sautuola is a famous case. De Sautuola was a Spanish gentleman, jurist, and 'amateur archaeologist' who faced extreme ridicule from the academics of his time. The elite French cave art community refused to acknowledge his findings simply because he was not part of their academic circle. In 1868, De Sautuola owned the land where the Altamira cave was found, and he began exploring it in 1875. Four years later, in 1879, he made a chance discovery that revealed the magnificent images of the famous Palaeolithic art galleries inside the caves of Altamira to the world, similar to those in Trois Frères and Lascaux. These caves had previously been undiscovered in the womb of the earth.

In the 1930s, Australian disputed anthropologist and 'amateur' archaeologist Frederick Slater suggested that there may be an even deeper connection between indigenous pictographs, ancient numbering systems, and Egyptian hieroglyphs. As with many amateur archaeologists, the academic community closes ranks and rejects their initial findings, only to find later that their theories, in whole or in part, have substance. Frederick Slater, whose ideas were well received and then rejected by the academic community, are now being re-visited by Cambridge University. In Darren Jordan's book, 'The Resurrection of Frederick Slater" published by Cambridge Scholars in 2018, Slater is described as:

> "...As a journalist Slater worked in the early 20th century in the NSW goldmining towns of Mudgee and Gulgong. It was probably here that he made friendships with Aboriginal people, possibly members of the Kamilaroi nation. Writing as a freelancer he showed a lot of interest in Aboriginal culture, writing a number of articles reflecting good research and positive attitudes towards Aboriginal people ... Slater represents an active amateur right on the edge of orthodox archaeology in the early 1930s. While he was

progressive and sympathetic to Aboriginal concerns and the protection of sites... working with ...the Australian Museum .... aligned against the stone collectors and amateurs, with the Museum representing a professional disciplinary interest in heritage conservation.... When he became a member of the Anthropological Society of NSW Slater found a more sceptical and better informed audience. He published a number of papers on the Aboriginal origins of place names in "Mankind."

Among the sites this ... group visited and recorded in the inter-war period was Burragurra or Devils Rock at Wollombi and another at Yango, both in the rugged sandstone country to the north of Sydney. These were major sites in size and setting, believed to be associated with men's initiation. Consistent with ethnographic observations of Aboriginal ceremony around the turn of the century,... the group believed that the symbols formed a narrative that was progressively revealed to initiates in the form of an unfolding story or stories (Howitt 1904 provides a helpful overview of contemporary understanding of the cosmology associated with initiation)

... although awareness of the complexity of Aboriginal society prior to the arrival of Europeans had been demonstrated by anthropologists ... were not inferior, either intellectually or in their evolutionary position to other cultures. He also reflects ... that myth and ritual were integral to a society's cultural transmission of ideas, and that symbols embedded deeper meanings, some of which were overt, while others may have been forgotten but remained present in relict form.... "Where Slater jumped beyond others was in the way he placed direct emphasis on the symbolism of the motifs becoming abstracted into concepts. A complex engraving site was therefore not read as a palimpsest of different motifs, nor as a cartoon sequence represented by motifs. Each shape - human form, footprint, shield, etc - was ... associated usually with a noun representing particular moral concepts. Therefore a rock engraving should be read simultaneously at a number of levels, firstly as a site within a geographic setting, secondly as a narrative produced by following the symbols and their sound values in the right sequence, thirdly as a sacred narrative unfolding as symbolic meanings are explained, and fourthly as a dictionary of higher meanings as symbols, that combined to produce new concepts and ideas."

Isaac Newton is not remembered for the stuff that he got wrong.

Similarly, some of Frederick Slater's ideas were too ambitious, but much of his work was groundbreaking and has been confirmed to be accurate. Today, it is widely accepted that the early indigenous people did travel from Africa to Australia and perhaps from Australia to other parts of the world. Slater's theories about the indigenous numbering system have also been proven to exist since the Palaeolithic era. Another amateur archaeologist discovered this, deciphering a "Lunar calendar" found in 20,000-year-old cave paintings in 2023, eighty-seven years after Slater first published his work.

Therefore, it is now easy to accept that early indigenous people had record-keeping systems equivalent to other ancient civilisations. Therefore, Slater's work should be recognised and appreciated by the academic community by and large.

Came From Africa To Australia

OUR BLACKS' ANCESTORS

SYDNEY, Saturday.

Ancestors of the Australian aboriginal left Africa approximately 150,000 years ago, claims Mr. Frederic Slater, well-known Sydney journalist and authority on the Australian aboriginal, in his book Scribes of the Stone Age, which has been accepted for publication in England.

Through succeeding years numbers of them accomplished their mighty journey to Australia, he holds. They walked from Africa by a land bridge. They were food-gatherers—they left Egypt before agriculture was dreamed of, and before Egyptians learned to write hieroglyphics, says Mr. Slater.

The Egyptians learned their system of hieroglyphics from the ancestors of our aborigines, and even the great Pythagoras derived many elements of his mathematics from a system originated by the forbears of the blackfellow.

YEARS OF RESEARCH

The book represents years of patient research. It contains 350 pictures and 80 plates, and is dedicated to the "Stone Age Men Who Still Exist."

Mr. Slater has been a student of the Australian aboriginal all his life, and is an authority on his language. By request, he has supplied native names for hundreds of Australian homes.

A few years ago he acquired a valuable aboriginal vocabulary, which opened up to him a hitherto unsuspected field of research.

The vocabulary is known as a "Murrigiwalda" (sacred language), and gave him the key to many avenues of investigation.

The vocabulary had been the property of Mrs. David Dunlop, wife of the first magistrate at Wollombi, near Cessnock, and contained clues to aboriginal rock-carvings, particularly some on the summits of mountains at Burragurra and Yango (Wollombi), which, Mr. Slater avers, were done by the blacks between 200 and 300 years ago.

WHAT CARVINGS TELL

These carvings and others in other parts of the State enabled Mr. Slater to arrive at conclusions concerning aboriginal paleography common to all parts of the world roamed by stone-age men. They shed new light on aboriginal numeration.

In his book, Mr. Slater seeks to prove that the stone-age aboriginal believed that men came from a protoplasm created by God as a special species, and that the original man could speak from the moment of his creation.

The author also offers evidence that the stone-age aborigine had a deep knowledge of the human circulatory system, that he believed that the origin of the planetary system was tidal, that he understood the creation of the world and knew much about light, darkness, fire.

Fresh evidence is also given that he believed in the immortality of the soul.

It is stated, too, that aspects of Mr. Slater's research will be of particular interest to students of the origin and history of Freemasonry.

A WORD ON COOK'S MAPPING OF AUSTRALIA

There are controversies surrounding James Tiberius Cook, an explorer, mathematician, and cartographer, not a coloniser.

In 1768, Admiral Sandwich organised a commission for Cook to be the commander of HMS Endeavour, which departed from England on 26 August. The Earl of Sandwich organised private funding, an old, refurbished flat-bottomed coal boat (The Endeavour), and some ancient Asian maps for Cook if he was interested in a journey of exploration and contact. They were idealists. Cook knew Admiral Sandwich through The Hellfire Club, of which they were both members. The club was introducing Hindu spirituality to England and helping women get the right to vote, for which the Church of England condemned all members to hell. This led to their popular nickname.

AS Cook's primary purpose was exploration and contact, the British government was unwilling to fund a peaceful exploratory mission. After all, this mysterious land had previously been claimed by the Dutch, the Portuguese, and the Spanish, who considered it too far and worthless to colonise. Their form of colonisation was to shoot first and ask questions later, and all locals they encountered were immediately enslaved. Happily, Cook and the Quaker offices on his boat were opposed to violence and slavery. However, on the day of his leaving, he was handed sealed royal orders to be opened when he was in Tahiti.

Joseph Banks requested to be included on this trip to document the botany. Banks, a nobleman, did not like Cook as he was just the son of a farmer. A commoner. His father's employer, Thomas Skottowe, paid for Cook to attend the local school. He had only five years of schooling but excelled. Banks created several problems for Cook on the voyage with his entitled elitist attitude. He unsuccessfully tried to size command of the expedition. It appears that Banks initiated the conflicts with the Indigenous Australians and Māori. Cook was left to stamp out the conflagrations lit by Banks. After the conflict, even when there had been a loss of life, Cook attempted and was successful at making reconciliations with the indigenous. Even after his death, he was so well respected in Hawaii. He was given a King's burial.

Cook arrived at Tahiti on April 13, 1769. There, he opened the sealed orders and found a royal order to search the South Pacific for signs of the postulated rich southern continent of Terra Australis and claim it in the name of George, the King of England. Cook, a Captain in the Royal Navy, had records that he received orders that he was not happy about.

However, he carried them out faithfully as it was his duty. He became the first person to circumnavigate Antarctica, a highly sought-after target for colonisation. After that, Cook sailed to New Zealand, circumnavigating and mapping the coastline. With the assistance of Tupaia, a Tahitian priest who had joined the expedition, Cook was the first European to communicate with the Māori people.

Cook was excited to see men in dark clothing and dark skin calmly observing his ships before he made landfall in Terra Australis. Noting in his journal:

> "... and were so near the shore as to distinguish several people upon the sea beach they appear'd to be of a very dark or black Colour but whether this was the real colour of their skins or the C[l]othes they have on I know not."

On 19 April 1770, Captain Cook and his team reached the southeastern coast of Australia near today's Point Hicks. This made them the first recorded Europeans to have encountered the eastern coastline of Australia. During their expedition, Cook had Sydney Parkinson, a ship's artist, detail the people, dwellings, clothing, and many people around the area, including Botany Bay. In his journal, Cook notes how well-tended and attractive the grounds around the bay were, almost like a garden rather than a farm. However, he was disappointed that the local inhabitants resisted contact. Two Gweagal men of the Dharawal / Eora nation opposed their landing, and in the confrontation, one of them was shot and wounded. Cook and his crew stayed at Botany Bay for a week, collecting water, timber, fodder and botanical specimens and exploring the surrounding area. Cook sought to establish relations with the local Indigenous population but failed. Sydney Parkinson was also a Quaker who opposed slavery and believed in the equality of all men.

This first landing site was later promoted by Joseph Banks in his own published account of the journey (not by James Cook) as a suitable candidate for situating a settlement and British colonial outpost.

Cook appeared enamoured with this idealistic place and noble but aloof people.

> "From what I have said of the Natives of New Holland they may appear to some to be the most wretched people upon earth, but in reality they are far more happier than we Europeans; being wholy unacquainted not only with the superfluous but the necessary conveniences so much sought after in Europe, they are happy in not knowing the use of them. They live in a Tranquillity which is not

disturb'd by the Inequality of the Condition. The Earth and sea of their own accord furnishes them with all things necessary for life; they covet not Magnificent Houses, Houshold-stuff. They live in a warm and fine Climate and enjoy a very wholsome Air, so that they have very little need of Clothing .... In short they seem'd to set no Value upon any thing we gave them, nor would they ever part with any thing of their own for any one article we could offer them; this, in my opinion argues that they think themselves provided with all the necessarys of Life and that they have no Superfluities"

According to his journals, he never claimed that this land was uninhabited.

During his voyage along the eastern coast of Australia in 1770, the HMB Endeavour landed fourteen times on the East Australian Coastline. None of his landings are celebrated as an Australian holiday. One of these landings was in Botany Bay, now part of New South Wales. The other 13 landings were made in the waters of Queensland. The fourteenth landing was on Booby Island, which is located to the west of Thursday Island. Besides these landing places, Cook also named 92 other landmarks on the East Coast, naming 106 places in total. Many of these place names are still in use today and would be familiar to the reader. It is worth mentioning that Cook did not name any landmarks after himself.

On the night of June 10th, 1770, the Endeavour ran aground on the Great Barrier Reef during a clear moonlit night. Captain Cook named the site Cape Tribulation and recorded the event in his journal.

"*... because here begun all our troubles.*"

The Endeavour suffered severe damage, and it took 23 hours of traumatic effort to pull the ship off the reef during high tide. After successfully heaving the boat off the reef, they managed to slow down the water leakage by utilising a technique called 'fothering'. This involved hauling a sail covered with oakum, dung and sheep's wool under the belly of the ship. With the leakage under control, they only needed to use one pump. However, it took them another week to find a safe harbour to repair the Endeavour. They spent seven weeks at Endeavour River for repairs. Banks and his team of botanists used this time to discover several natural history wonders previously unknown to science. During their exploration, they found a significant portion of the Endeavour's East Coast botanical collection. This period at Endeavour River was Cook's expedition's most extended land base. The crew gathered food by fishing and collecting giant clams and turtles. They also discovered green vegetables and yams to add to their diet. During their stay, they ate kangaroo meat for the first time after observing the indigenous people hunting them and realising they were edible animals.

When the crew of the Endeavour made contact with the Guugu Yimithirr people from north of the harbour, they learned that the name of the mysterious beast they had seen was "ganguuru," which they interpreted as "kangaroo." During this first meaningful contact between Indigenous people and Europeans, Parkinson recorded 130 words and phrases of the Guugu Yimithirr language in his Journal. This was the first written record of an Indigenous language in the country, including the names of nine individuals. They had six meetings with the Guugu Yimithirr,

During one visit, an altercation occurred when Captain Cook refused to share the turtles caught by the ship's crew. Unaware of the local culture, the crew did not know that catching a turtle meant a feast day that was shared with everyone. This refusal to share the turtles insulted the locals, and they were chased away from the camp after twice setting fire to it. The fire destroyed everything around the camp and even killed a suckling pig. In self-defence, Cook wounded one man with a musket shot. He regretted this, so he ran after them into the bush. Members of his crew ran after him to help him. He followed the group until they reached a rocky bar called Reconciliation Rocks. After exchanging peace signs, Cook, along with Joseph Banks and several other individuals, returned some spears to the elders of the group, who then sat down with them. Cook wrote in his journal:
> "... we now return'd the darts we had taken from them, which reconciled every thing."

Parkinson confirmed this by adding in his journal:
> "... Several of them came to us afterwards and made peace..."

The Endeavour returned to England shortly after that.

On May 13, 1787, the "First Fleet" departed from Portsmouth, England, with 1400 people on board. Most were British, but there were also a few Americans, French, Irish, Brazilians, and Africans. They were in a hurry. They needed to get to Australia to set up a colony before the Dutch, the Portuguese, or the Spanish returned to set up their colonies as they had done in the Americas. The colonising group included military leaders, sailors, tradesmen, cooks and 700 indentured convict slaves. On January 18, 1788, the fleet arrived at Botany Bay, but Governor Arthur Phillip rejected it as a site for the new colony. The bay was shallow, lacked an ample supply of fresh water, and the land needed to be fertile. Instead, they chose Port Jackson (Sydney Harbour) to the north, where they arrived and raised their flag on January 26, 1788.

Captain James Cook had passed away ten years before this event. He would have rolled over in his grave to learn that his beloved Terra Australia had been declared Terra Nullus by Joseph Banks and the colonists who followed his advice, not Cook's, 17 years after he mapped the coastline. Maybe, just maybe, we are angry at the wrong man for the terror, genocide and excuses that colonisation brought to this country and its indigenous people.

> *Anyone can become angry… That is easy. But to be angry with the right person, to the right degree, at the right time, for the right purpose, and in the right way—that is not easy. The prudent man aspires not to pleasure, but to the absence of pain.* Aristotle

It is sometimes appropriate to feel angry in response to a situation. However, a wise person will only get angry when it is justified and will not act foolishly in their anger. They will not let other people influence their anger but will gather all the facts themselves. They will be in control of their anger rather than allowing their anger to control them.

Cook's admonition to not settle New Holland:

> *"…in short, most of the large Trees in this Country are of a hard and ponderous nature and could not be applied to many purposes… But, the Country itself so far as we know doth not produce any one thing that can become an Article in trade to invite Europeans to fix a settlement upon it,.."* Captain JT Cook

IN THE END

In the end, it will be the same as in the beginning.

The indigenous people will still be here.

The dreaming and the dreamtime will still be here.

The land will still feed us and supply our needs.

We will still have the same land, the same ancestor spirits, the same totems that created this land and all life, and indeed, the whole universe;

They will still show us how little we need and how happy we can be.

They will still tell us the stories of the laws of existence that we need to survive.

Will you follow those rules and survive?

Can we agree to live by the five maxims of this land?

1. *'We don't own the land; the land owns us.'*
2. *'The Land is my mother; my mother is the land.'*
3. *'The land is our food, our culture, our spirit and identity.'*
4. *'We don't have boundary fences; we have spiritual connections.'*
5. *'Land is the beginning and the end. It is where we start, and it is where we will ALL go.'*

Left: Donnie Didge, receiving his 'Indigenous Citizen of the Year' Award 2013
Above: Aboriginal Dance Workshop at Highfields Pioneer Village 2018

Photos used with permission of Don Nikkelson.

Below: Shé D'Montford (author/organiser) with indigenous elders from Australia, Ireland and The U.S. 'On Country' Dunn's Swamp 2011

**I know, you're reading the back page first – everybody does.
So, here's a quick summary:**

With interest rates skyrocketing, wouldn't it be good to be able to eat for FREE?

The Indigenous Australians have been living off the fat land since the beginning of time.

Before banks, before supermarkets, there was Bushtucker. Indigenous culture flourished.

This is the perfect time to learn the art of living close to nature to recession-proof yourself.

To understand how to live in harmony with the land according to indigenous culture, examining their etiquette, dreaming, magick

and food

is essential.

If you really want to make a friend, go to someone's house and eat with him… the people who give you their food give you their heart.

CESAR CHAVEZ

Share the Love.

If you love this book, send it to a friend.

See our other magickal titles on
www.happymediumpublishing.org.au
Happy Medium Publishing
+61(0)402 793 604

www.ingramcontent.com/pod-product-compliance
Lightning Source LLC
Chambersburg PA
CBHW050436010526
44118CB00013B/1550